LIVES
of the
SAINTS
YOU
SHOULD
KNOW
VOLUME 2

LIVES
of the
SAINTS
YOU
SHOULD
KNOW

VOLUME 2

MARGARET & MATTHEW
BUNSON

Our Sunday Visitor Publishing Division
Our Sunday Visitor, Inc.
Huntington, Indiana 46750

ISBN: 0-87973-753-0
LCCCN: 94-67356

Cover design by Rebecca J. Heaston
Illustrations by Margaret Bunson

PRINTED IN THE UNITED STATES OF AMERICA

753

This book is dedicated, with appreciation and respect,
to Father Graham McDonnell
of the Good Shepherd Movement in Kyoto, Japan,
and to Father Ryogo Yuki, S.J.,
of the 26 Martyrs Museum in Nagasaki, Japan.

Contents

Oh, how glorious
is the kingdom
where all the saints
rejoice with Christ;
clothed in white robes,
they follow the Lamb
withersoever he goeth.

Magnificat Antiphon
Feast of All Saints

Introduction

This second volume of *Lives of the Saints You Should Know* seeks to provide further demonstration of the universality of the Church by offering once more to the reader the examples and the achievements of some very remarkable souls. These individuals came from a host of varying backgrounds and lived in many different eras. Some were of common birth, others were born into noble families, and one was even a king. They were mystics and missionaries, laypersons and members of the clergy. Each, however, gave witness to the Catholic faith and is deserving of the veneration bestowed upon him or her by the Church and its members.

As was discussed in volume one of this series, the word saint is derived from the Latin term *sanctus*, meaning "holy" or "consecrated," and the Church over the years has established a careful and very complete system for determining whether someone is truly worthy of the honor of being called a saint. This system is known as the process of canonization. It was first established by Innocent III (who was pope from 1199 to 1216), but the method we know today was put into place in 1634. The first person ever to be declared formally (or officially) a saint was Ulrich of Augsburg, who was canonized all the way back in 993 by Pope John XV. Before him, though, many men and women were honored as saints, especially those who had died as martyrs for the faith.

It might be useful to remember here the different terms used for persons on their way to canonization. "Venerable" is used for those considered possible candidates for later advancement to sainthood. Some individuals bear the title Venerable but will not become saints for whatever reason; this does not mean, though, that they were not holy and deserving of our honor. "Blessed" is used for those who have been "beatified" (or proven to have lived virtuously and to have merited the eternal rewards of heaven); they are often destined for canonization in time. "Saint" is the title bestowed on the individual in the final stage of canonization. It is the official seal of approval by the Church, marking the person worthy of veneration by all the faithful.

Veneration, of course, does not mean adoration, since adoration is reserved exclusively for God.

It should also be remembered that these special people help form what is called the "Communion of Saints," the spiritual connection between the saints in heaven, the souls in purgatory, and the living on earth. Saints additionally serve as protectors and patrons of various places, countries, and people, as well as many different professions, such as painters, policemen, doctors, writers, and students. Simply put, saints are always there, giving encouragement and offering their prayers that everyone might join them in the eternal happiness of heaven.

Margaret and Matthew Bunson

Ansgar

Chapter 1

Ansgar

Saint Ansgar is called the "Apostle of the North" and the "Apostle of Scandinavia," which means that he chose to leave his comfortable and safe monastery to preach in one of the cruelest, most brutal, and most pagan regions to be found on the earth at the time. The people of the North, the men and women of Scandinavia, were the Horrible Hagars of their era: They were known variously as the Norse, the Northmen, or the Vikings. The names didn't mean much, because other peoples were terrified of them no matter what they were called. So feared were these warriors that most people ran for their lives when they heard that the Norse (or Northmen or Vikings) were in the neighborhood. So dreaded were these roving bands of destroyers that European Christians prayed daily: *A furore normanorum libera nos, Domine* ("From the fury of the Norsemen, deliver us O Lord!").

The Northmen were hardy warriors who sailed out of the frozen wastes of their homelands in Norway, Denmark, and Sweden to bring death, slavery, and destruction to their southern European neighbors and to anyone else who strayed across their dreaded paths. Muscular, battle-trained, and filling the air with the war chants of their pagan gods Thor and Odin, the Vikings used sleek, fast ships that carried them through storms and winds, mists and fogs — the kind of weather that kept saner people at home. They wielded swords, shields, and battle-axes, and some were known to go "berserk" in battle. This means that they became so excited by hand-to-hand combat that they felt no wounds or pain until their enemies had been slain. It soon became quite clear to everyone else in Europe that someone that crazy makes a dangerous opponent in a war.

The Norsemen were very set in their ways, believing in their gods, their battles, and the open seas, to which they gave marvelous names, such as "whale-road." Now as one might imagine, these hard-bitten fighters were not exactly thrilled to hear Ansgar talking about peace, charity, love, and brotherhood; but he preached to them anyway, opening the door for other Friends of God. Called Anskar in some historical records, the saint spent most of his life in Denmark and Sweden, turning his back on honors and comfort in order to perform his mission: to bring the light of the faith to lands that had never known the Good News of salvation.

Ansgar was born in Amiens, in modern France, in A.D. 801, and he was a member of a noble family of the area. He was not the oldest son of the family, obviously, because he did not inherit titles or lands, as was then the custom. Actually, as the second or third son of a noble house, Ansgar did not count for much in society or even in his own family. In the thinking of that era, it was important for a nobleman to give his heir all of his lands as well as the titles that his ancestors had accumulated (or gotten) — lawfully or otherwise — over the centuries. A baron or local ruler always kept his holdings together, no matter what happened to the family. If you divided your land among your sons, then the whole territory became weakened. Oftentimes, sons would squabble with one another or worse yet, start wars with each other, raising unwilling armies of peasants and generally wrecking the neighborhood. In the wake of such mindless wars and fighting, the once strong and proud land could be attacked by neighbors, bringing about the collapse of the family line and everything that generations of the nobles had built.

The need to keep lands in one heir's hands was certainly good news if you were the firstborn, but it was not much fun to be the second, third, or fourth son. Their lot was sometimes miserable. One had to serve one's older brothers, help take care of castles or forts, knowing that at any moment one might be married off to some other family to forge an alliance. Young sons had few other ways of making a living in the world. There was always military service, of course. Any young man crazy enough to enter the army of a local lord could earn riches and fame, but he had to manage to live long enough to enjoy them, which was very difficult back then. Most families, however, frowned upon "swords for hire" in their midst. One solution as to what to do with one's youngest son was to send him to join a monastery; this was a convenient solution for daughters, too.

The custom of putting younger sons, as well as some daughters, into monasteries and convents was considered perfectly logical by noble or high-ranking parents of that day and age. To begin with, such parents would not have to support these sons, and would not have to provide a dowry for the daughters. The monastery was considered a better solution.

If such a son stayed in the monastic life, he could not upset everyone by demanding a share of the family properties. At the same time, however, the lad dumped on the doorstep of an abbey or monastery could expect to have a decent career in the Church and stood a good chance of making something of himself if he tried. Lastly, parents who presented their sons to the Church as "oblates" or "gifts" believed that they would be rewarded for their generosity.

Such "oblates" had to be physically strong, rational (or sane), and capable of being educated. The monasteries of that era were beacons of knowledge and culture in the world, especially considering the fact that not too many people around them could even write their own names. When signing contracts they made an X. Such people remained tied to the lands, without schooling, and even members of the aristocracy often were illiterate, which means they had to have secretaries to read them the "morning papers." The monasteries and convents conducted schools for the lucky ones considered worth educating. The monks and nuns of these institutions of the Church preserved the old manuscripts, making copies and studying them so that new generations would benefit from the past. Not only scriptural knowledge and revelations were preserved but art, music, science, and history as well.

Ansgar arrived at the Benedictine Abbey of Corbie, called "Old Corbie" in some records, located near his family estates. His adjustment to his new life did not take long, mainly because he was a practical fellow who understood life in his times. He loved God and had been entrusted into the hands of another saint, Paschasius Radbertus, a brilliant scholar who trained Ansgar in the spiritual life. God had chosen Ansgar! He was not just an extra child to be discarded but a rare human being who would open the pathways of faith in the frozen wastes of northern Europe.

After growing up in the Benedictine order, being ordained and taking his vows as a monk, Ansgar and some of his monastic companions were transferred to "New Corbie," an abbey designed to serve the Saxons of Westphalia, Germany. This "New Corbie" soon became a haven for scholars who studied many of the arts and sciences, imparting knowledge to anyone who cared to listen to them, attracting many and influencing the entire region.

One rather exalted person drawn to "New Corbie" and to Ansgar was Harald, king of Denmark. He had been forced into exile by political events in his homeland and had taken refuge in the court of Emperor Louis the Pious, the son and heir of the famed Charlemagne. The exiled king found Ansgar to be sane, charming, and steadfast in the faith, and when he received an invitation to return to the throne of Denmark, he asked Ansgar to go with him, to bring Christ to the Norsemen and their families. After Ansgar received permission from his superiors, he set sail for cold lands unknown.

At first Ansgar found himself preaching to empty houses and churches. His message of peace, brotherhood, and love fell on deaf ears, and he was lucky to escape from some places with his body in one piece. The Vikings believed that the virtues he spoke about were weaknesses in human beings, bound to bring them attacks from stronger tribes. These warriors and their relatives cared deeply for one another, but they had no intention of running about doing good for total strangers or enemies because they were convinced that such actions would court disaster. A battle-ax across the skull was the only greeting Vikings wanted to give to most people they met on their travels. They also had no desire to spare the churches that fell into their hands, as they wanted to kill priests and nuns along with other invaded populations because such people often were the protectors of priceless treasures.

Ansgar did convert some of the Danes, although many chiefs fought against the Christian faith and made their dislike of him evident. These chiefs had powers because of the old gods and the old ways, and they pointed to the fact that the ancient traditions of the region had served them well over the years. Ansgar was a foreigner, talking about an unknown religion and introducing new ideas as well. Love, equality, kindness, goodness, and peace were not exactly part of the Viking way of life.

A Christian school was established by Ansgar in southern Denmark, standing as a symbol for the great saints of Scandinavia, such as Bridget of Sweden, who would follow the Apostles of the North. Ansgar opened the school, saw it staffed and financially secure, and then set sail for Bridget's land. There were Norsemen waiting for him and his fellow ship passengers, and they were not there to bid Ansgar a friendly good-bye.

The northern seas were virtually crawling with pirates in those days. Sleek ships roamed up and down the usual shipping lanes and overtook the slower passenger vessels. Ansgar's ship was attacked, but he escaped. The details of his adventures are lost in history, but the poor man must have suffered as he made his way to Birka, the Swedish capital at the time. There he was welcomed by King Bjorn. Another man in the royal court, a powerful councilor named Herigar, was even more enthusiastic about Ansgar's arrival. Herigar built Sweden's first Christian church on one of his own estates.

After this initial success, Ansgar received word from his superiors that he was to return to Germany. Setting sail once again, and probably looking over his shoulder all the way, Ansgar returned to his monastery to discover that he had been appointed as the archbishop of Hamburg. This was in 831, and Hamburg was a thriving city that would demand Ansgar's time and energies. He was not thrilled about the appointment because honors and ranks meant nothing to him. Also, he knew that God had destined him for the northern missions, whether the Vikings wanted him there or not. His name meant "God's Spear," and that seemed to demonstrate Ansgar's true work in the world. Pope Gregory IV agreed and named Ansgar the papal legate to the North. The saint would have to learn how to divide his time between duties, something that would demand spectacular juggling of time, energy, and graces.

As a human being, Ansgar was known for his charity, firmness, and "asceticism" (a word meaning that he had few pleasures). He preferred bread and water and spent his time on his knees before God. These descriptions were given by his contemporaries, who admired him and his missions. He also managed a miracle or two along the way, gaining a reputation and earning himself many critics.

People who cannot perform miracles, especially those who do not believe in God with any real enthusiasm, like to make fun of anyone capable of bringing about supernatural cures or conversions. Such people roll their eyes when they hear about miracles and then recite a whole list of scientific reasons why such things could not have taken place. There are people who do not believe in anything they cannot touch, hear, or see for themselves. They will go along with all sorts of really crazy political or social ideas, but they laugh at supernatural matters. This is logical, of course. If such men and women admit that miracles are possible, they have to admit the existence of God. If God exists, they in turn have to lead lives of faith, and for some that is difficult. It is easier for such individuals to deny everything but the material world and the flesh.

Responding to his critics, Ansgar said simply: "Were God to choose to do such things, I would ask him for one miracle only — that by his power he would make me a good man." That, of course, silenced everyone, and Ansgar went about his work in peace. Who could argue with that attitude? For the remaining years of his life, he divided his time between Hamburg and the North, spending years in both locations and hours on board small ships trying to outrun the pirates. Then disaster struck when the Norseman paid him an unexpected call, making an appearance that Ansgar and his neighbors could have done without.

In 845, a vast fleet of Norwegian ships (some historical records number them at six hundred) arrived in Hamburg. That city was located on the Elbe and Alster Rivers, which made it vulnerable to any ships arriving as an attack force. The people of Hamburg — as well as Ansgar — heard the warnings given about the approaching armada. Some wailed and began praying. Others fainted or ran around like deranged, or crazy, chickens. Most packed up their belongings and fled inland to the nearby city of Bremen. The Norsemen did not bother to chase the refugees. They were too busy murdering and enslaving the people who did not get away. Also, the city had many fine treasures, enough to make the raid worthwhile. The Norwegians left no stone unturned in their hunt for riches, and it would take the people of Hamburg many years to restore their once-beautiful city.

Ansgar had to repair the cathedral and begin the reconstruction of Hamburg because that was what archbishops did to their churches and cities in those days. He returned to the ruins the instant the Norwegians had set sail, and he set up committees and work groups to look for survivors in the rubble and to start normal services for the locals. It took him years to accomplish the restoration of Hamburg and to reopen trade and financial affairs. He also had to comfort those who had survived the raid, people who were convinced that the end of the world was just around the corner. Survivors of such disasters do tend to be out of sorts for a while. During this time the city of Bremen was given into his care as well, only adding to his many burdens.

In 854, Ansgar returned to Denmark and Sweden. While he was there, many converts were baptized, including Erik, the king of the area called Jutland. The seeds of the faith had been sown but at the cost of Ansgar's energies. He worked until 865, when the people of the North, and his own Hamburg, mourned his passing. He was followed by Rimbert, his assistant, who became the Second Apostle of the North. The Church celebrates Saint Ansgar's feast day on February 3.

Chapter 2

Brigid

Ireland is an island just to the west of Great Britain in the Atlantic Ocean, separated not only by two channels and the Irish Sea but by centuries of faith and traditions. Many call Ireland the Emerald Isle, the Isle of Destiny, or Erin. In the past the island had many other interesting names as well: Ierna, Hibernia, Ogygia, Inisfail, Banba, and Scotia. A beautiful land, Ireland has always had mysteries, traditions, legends, and some of the world's most interesting personalities walking through its lovely landscapes.

Saint Patrick brought Christianity to Ireland around 432, returning there after having escaped from slavery on the island as a lad, and following in the footsteps of another missionary, Saint Palladius. The faith spread quickly because Patrick knew the traditions of the Irish people, remembering what he learned during his years as a slave. Now the return of Patrick to the very place where his life had been made miserable is a remarkable example of his charity and zeal. Putting to use all that he had learned at the hands of his Irish captors demonstrates Patrick's practical approach to his apostolic mission. Escaping from his bondage, he did not turn to pleasures or rest but became a priest and returned to Ireland to bring the Irish the word of Christ. Wherever Patrick went he was able to convert people and to build parish churches. In time, of course, these parishes were joined into dioceses, and bishops and other officials were appointed to guide them.

These prelates, a fancy name for bishops and other high-ranking priests, met in synods occasionally to decide matters of importance and pressing issues that arose as the Church in Ireland expanded. At one such synod, or gathering of prelates, a bishop named Ibor received a vision in a dream. He was not used to having such revelations, apparently, because he felt a compelling need to tell his experience to anyone who would listen to him in the synod. When Ibor and his fellow bishops were gathered in a hall completing the day's synodal business, he announced the details of what he had seen in his revelation. The prelate then told everyone around him that Blessed Mary would come to the Gaels, the Irish people.

What the other churchmen thought about Ibor's astounding announcement was never recorded by the historians of the time. Before anyone could make some sort of comment, in fact, a small nun entered the hall through a rear door. Bishop Ibor turned to look at her and then leaped right out of his chair and started pointing at the nun in a state of absolute shock. Ibor shouted in a loud voice: "That is the woman that I saw in my dream!"

Now the nun may have been a stranger to Ibor, but a good many other bishops present recognized her with ease. She was Saint Brigid, honored ever after as the "Mary of the Gaels." She is sometimes called Saint Bride, and in 1962 was named a patroness of Ireland, sharing that distinction with Saint Patrick himself.

Bishop Ibor was not the only Gael who related stories about Brigid while she was alive, and upon her death people started remembering all kinds of strange tales. Legends and rumors were very much a part of life in that time, because people did not have many diversions or amusements. The highlight of a festival was the arrival of a bard, who strummed on a lute or harp and sang about the fallen heroes of the past. That was logical. The present wasn't very encouraging, so it was better to look back to the time of the great ones. Bards went from village to village, reminding people of better days gone by.

Brigid lived in a turbulent (or violence-filled) era in history, a period in which only the strong survived, a time of men and women who were known for their strengths and spirit of independence. She was born in A.D. 450 or 453, in the era that witnessed the collapse of the Roman Empire in the West. She was the daughter of a slave named Brocca and the Irish chieftain of Leinster, Dubthach.

Brocca, probably young and reasonably attractive, served in Dubthach's court in Faughart, Lauth, and she attracted his attention, whether she wanted it or not. The slaves had precious little say about their fates in good times or in bad, especially when a chieftain was involved. Saint Patrick, remembering his own years as a slave, called the suffering of the women slaves "the greatest of all." Brocca fit into this category, so she had little say about anything, including love.

The chieftain may have fathered a child by the slave Brocca, but he felt no obligation because of that fact to raise the mother of his child to a new and exalted status. Brocca probably remained a slave or received manumission, which is a fancy word for being set free. In the case of her daughter, Brigid, however, people had to give the child a certain amount of respect and courtesy as the offspring of a powerful chief. Thus Brigid grew up between two worlds, that of her mother's bondage, or low status, and that of her father's court. The court, of course, was filled with nobles and various levels of high-ranking servants. None of these people would have taken up a collection or signed a petition asking that Brigid be brought to the king's presence or showered with fine clothes.

Brigid was just another child in their eyes and promptly forgotten, particularly because she had no claims to the wealth of the chieftain and his family. Brigid survived her infancy and then was allowed to remain in peace. She appears to have spent much time on a farm with her mother, as no call to an honored place came from Dubthach or his aristocratic relatives. Actually, the farm was the safest place for Brigid, who would have been badly treated, or exposed to the sort of pleasures that people used to pass the time in those days. Life on the farms of that period was tuned to the seasons, to the growing patterns of life, and to the worship of God.

Brocca and the child stayed on a farm that was probably part of the chieftain's estate. Brigid was raised as a devout Christian, since both of her parents had been baptized by the great Saint Patrick personally. The chieftain appears to have forgotten much of what Patrick taught him, but Brocca found her faith serving as a shield against life itself. She remained a Christian and took care to raise Brigid with the same sort of zeal. Thus in the quiet rural life, amid Ireland's scenic splendors and the parade of the seasons, Brigid's faith flowered into genuine strength. She grew up happy, strong in her personality, and filled with the compassion that would mark her character in later years. That compassion probably gave Brocca many a fit, at least an uncomfortable moment or two.

Even as a small girl Brigid had concern for the poor, and when she saw anyone in need she gave that person everything in her possession. Now slaves had very little that they could give away, at least not without having to make an accounting to some harsh overseer or to a master. If Brigid was handing over all that they owned to every stranger limping down the side of a hill, she and Brocca were headed for a great deal of trouble. The child probably had a heart-to-heart talk with her mother rather early on, and in this conversation learned the facts about life, about their true status in the area, and about the dangers of giving everything they possessed to strangers. Actually, one cannot give away something that one does not have. Brocca must have explained that they had nothing, and even more cruel, she was a piece of property herself, owned by the chieftain. What Brigid thought of that situation when she realized it, was not recorded. Likely enough she must have made the best of a bad situation and set about her tasks.

She obviously didn't continue to give away the store, because the two women endured on the farm, and she grew in grace and in faith. Brigid resolved at a very young age to give herself to Christ, which quite simply meant to embrace the religious life as a nun.

She received the veil, the symbol of the convent, from Saint Macaille, an apostle to the Gaels who followed in Saint Patrick's hallowed footsteps. There is no way of knowing just what her chieftain father thought about that act of consecration. Maybe he did not care one way or another, or maybe he thought it better to have no opinion at all. He would have had to be a brave man to stand against Macaille, who could be ferocious about matters of the faith and was well known for facing down any opponent. Saint Mel of Armagh, yet another holy missionary, received Brigid's final vows after her years of training in the spiritual life. Both Mel and Macaille spent their time providing this extraordinary young woman with the spiritual truths, with the discipline of a religious, and with insight into the nature of the soul called to a special ministry. They recognized a remarkable spirit, and they nurtured Brigid's virtues as Almighty God filled her with grace. The two saints also undertook the training of Brigid and her companions as they started a convent and a new religious congregation.

In 468, however, Mel was transferred to Kildare, then called Cill-Dara, the Church of the Oak. There Brigid founded a double-abbey, an important monastery that allowed men and women to become religious members. They lived separately, of course, but they were all under the authority of Brigid. She was Ireland's first abbess, which must have come as a shock to a lot of people, and she brought her visions not only to her monastery but to the entire area. To safeguard the abbey, Brigid chose Saint Conleth to serve as spiritual director, as the one who set the standards for behavior, study, and day-to-day operations of the large institution.

When the monastery rose as a beautiful symbol of the Church in Kildare, people quite naturally began to build their homes and shops nearby. A cathedral was erected, and Kildare prospered not only as a spiritual and religious center but as a sign of a renaissance for all of Erin.

The great art school started by Brigid as part of the monastic mission only added to Kildare's fame across the land. The Gaelic, or Celtic, artistic styles were very sophisticated and beautiful. Brigid welcomed anyone interested in carrying on the traditions of the past, the exquisite artistic styles that had brought the Gaels such honors among many peoples. One noted result was the *Book of Kildare*, a volume of spiritual matters so wonderfully illuminated in the style of the period that some early critics claimed that no human being could have managed to produce such a masterpiece. The book, they announced, was made by angels as they watched over Brigid in her prayers.

If all this was not enough, Saint Brigid also kept a strange menagerie — a collection of animals — in the Kildare Abbey. She had a wild boar there, complete with ferocious tusks, beady eyes, and probably a somewhat nasty temper, as wild boars are not known for their winning ways! A fox cub and other exotic creatures lived alongside the boar, and wild ducks came into the compound whenever Brigid invited them for lunch.

Now all this artistic work and love of nature were fine and good, because they clearly demonstrate the role of the Church in times of human suffering and ignorance. The Church in the monasteries and convents served as genuine islands of knowledge and kept alive the beautiful and good things about human development. Kildare was a beacon in a very dreary and dark period of world history. Brigid, however, was a working abbess who was responsible for the spiritual training and direction of countless other souls. She administered a vast estate and the lives of hundreds of pious men and women.

She also received the ragged armies of the poor at the abbey gate, giving each individual a cup of milk and a piece of warm fresh-baked bread. Clothes and blankets were probably collected and distributed as well, since the weather could turn damp and cold without warning.

Brigid, described by her contemporaries as strong and happy, had compassion on everyone, and her acts of kindness became well known throughout the land. People spoke about her good works, adding a word or two here and there, until a whole series of legends circulated in Ireland. One such legend stated that Brigid's cows always gave milk three times a day so that she would always have something for the poor. Another tradition claims that even glasses of water given to the poor at the abbey turned into milk, just because Brigid worried so about those men, women, and children who were in need.

A mention of Brigid in the *Book of Lismore*, a document dating to her era, is a bit more enthusiastic. That book tells the world that Brigid "helped all in danger; stopped pestilence, the rage of the storm of the sea." The *Book of Lismore* also called her "the Prophetess of Christ."

The great abbey and the poor and the sick were Brigid's main concerns, but she also kept an eye on the dying, especially those who had not accepted Christ. A well-known pagan chieftain took to his bed, with his family keeping vigil, as everyone knew that he was sinking fast. Brigid appeared at the house and offered to sit with the chieftain. No one refused her entry because of her fame and because of her concern. Brigid took a chair and calmly sat beside the chief, reaching down to gather rushes from the floor.

The custom of putting rushes — narrow reeds or fresh grasses — on the floors or castles and commoner's cottages, lasted a long time in many parts of the world. The rushes served as disposable carpets, becoming matted and dirty in a short time. People dropped food on the floor, tracked in mud from the fields and lanes, and allowed their untrained dogs to use the floors as latrines. After a day or so, of course, the rushes were glued together, forming a foul-smelling mass. They were then gathered up and thrown away, and new, fresh rushes were laid on the floor.

Obviously there were fresh ones beside the bed of the pagan chieftain, as Brigid gathered a few and started forming them into the shape of a cross. The dying chieftain, intrigued by Brigid and her odd preoccupation with rushes, asked her what she was doing. The saintly abbess was only too happy to explain, and as she had a gift with words, she kept the man spellbound. He converted and died in the faith, and ever after the Irish have kept the tradition of hanging rush crosses in their barns and houses on Brigid's feast day.

Thus the years passed in Kildare, with Brigid administering the abbey and taking care of all in need. She never stopped serving others, as she never halted her prayers of praise. She died on February 1, in 523 or 525, and was buried in the Kildare Cathedral. Her remains were removed from the cathedral in 878, when a Viking raid on the area threatened all that was holy and dear.

Downpatrick, the burial site of Saint Patrick and Saint Columba, became Saint Brigid's final resting place. Brigid's feast day is February 1, and besides being the patroness of Ireland, she is also the protectress of poets, fugitives, blacksmiths, dairymaids, newborn babies, and cattle.

Catherine of Siena

Chapter 3

Catherine of Siena

A six-year-old girl was walking through the streets of the great city of Siena one fine day, led gently, hand in hand, by her brother after a visit to the house of a relative. As the two passed the Church of Saint Dominic, near their home, the girl looked up and saw Christ and his Apostles Peter, Paul, and John watching her from the sky. The vision changed her life forever, for like most sensible people she responded to the sight of the Savior and the saints in the great blue yonder. Such heavenly beings do not suddenly loom up in the sky without good reason. The human individual witnessing them should be prepared for special graces and for special tasks that must be performed in the name of God's will. That six-year-old child being visited by the vision over the church was Catherine Benincasa. In time she would be known as Saint Catherine of Siena, a Doctor of the Church and one of the greatest saints honored by the faithful.

When Catherine's brother Stephen brought her home and started to explain how they were returning from the house of a married sister when something startled the child, the family gathered around excitedly. Their mother, Lapa, listened calmly and then restored order and probably sat the two of them down to the table to distract them with food. Catherine was the youngest child of the family, the twenty-fifth (yes, number twenty-five!), having been born to Lapa and her husband, Giacomo, on March 25, 1347.

The family was comfortable enough to raise more than two dozen offspring, and Lapa apparently welcomed them, one and all. Giacomo, who dyed cloths and material for a living, belonged to "the Party of the Twelve." This was a union of middle-class tradesmen and minor officials who stood firm in a very dangerous period of time in Italy. In the city of Siena, for example, groups revolted and brought down the local government whenever they felt like it. When the authorities were run out of town, the people of Siena looked to "the Party of the Twelve" for common sense and continuity. Someone had to keep things running, and this group had managed city affairs several times, which meant that any idiot could start a revolution at the drop of a hat knowing that the union of merchants would keep things going smoothly, no matter how many nuts ran through the streets.

The incident, as odd as it was, might have become just a memory if Catherine had returned to her old self again. Instead, she changed, praying in private, trying to avoid conversation, and fasting. This, of course, was a normal response to the great spiritual favor shown to her; but her mother, Lapa, felt anxious about it all. Catherine's mother was normally addressed as Mona Lapa, the same title given to the painting of a smiling woman called Lisa. "Mona" was a title of respect, having nothing to do with nobility or legal titles.

Mona Lapa, having raised two dozen other sons and daughters, put up with Catherine for about two weeks and then made her live more normally so that other family members and friends would not think she had lost her mind. The mother was uneasy, however, because Catherine was not the sort of child who needed to be in the spotlight or one who put on airs. Lapa had the strange sensation that she was dealing with something quite beyond the pranks of a wayward six-year-old who had been the victim of a trauma, or shock.

As Catherine entered her teens, of course, the situation became worse. To begin with, Catherine stayed home all day and all night. The custom at the time, carried out in Siena and in other regions, demanded that all young women older than twelve could not go out without an escort. Most marriages were arranged for these teenage damsels, so they were whisked away from their homes. Catherine refused even to think about marriage. When her parents, in desperation, agreed that she could go into a convent, Catherine declined that idea as well.

At the age of sixteen, Catherine asked to become a member of the Dominican Tertiaries (or the Third Order), especially designed for men and women living in the world. Members wore the Dominican habit (robes in this case) and kept to a schedule of prayer and good works. Catherine, a handsome young woman, did not exactly fit the usual description of Tertiaries in Siena.

Most of the people involved in the Third Order in Siena were elderly women who had remained unmarried or widowed at the time. The thought of a teenager being among them did not fill them with any great enthusiasm, and many wondered why she was asking for membership in their order. The women debated Catherine's request with the local Dominican clergy and then relented. They agreed to allow the young woman a term of probation, a time in which she could prove herself worthy of their calling.

Catherine received the robes of the Third Order and retired to a room to pray and fast, leaving that refuge only to attend Mass and other services. Her confessor was the only person she spoke to, and she lived on bread and water as well as various herbs.

Interiorly, meaning inside her heart and soul, Catherine was maturing in a spiritual sense, discovering the way humans can experience loneliness, a sense of rejection and dryness, followed by the consolations of visions and prayer. She was learning a valuable lesson of the mystical life, one shared by the great contemplative saints: "Love the God of Consolation, not the consolations of God."

After three years, Catherine realized she had a mission in the world that was quite different than she had imagined. As a result, she came out of her room and began to undertake the work of the Third Order members. She joined these women in visiting hospitals and prisons, and she went to the homes of the poor. She was living at home, eating very little except for the Blessed Sacrament, something that drove Mona Lapa almost wild; but everyone who saw her remarked about the joy and radiance evident in her face.

Her family lived in a solid middle-class neighborhood, called Fontebranda, and this became a very busy place as Catherine's fame grew. Slowly a small group of Dominican priests, nobles, and men and women from all walks of life gathered around her. They knew that some people resented her lifestyle and her charm, calling her the "Queen of Fontebranda." Others were not so generous in their opinions, dismissing her as a witch.

Such ugly remarks, however, were said carefully because Catherine's friends and allies, whom she called her "children," were among the most powerful families in the city. They aided her when she went to sit with the representatives of feuding groups and made them negotiate, or come to terms with their differences. This sort of meditation, or serving as a referee in the ongoing arguments, earned her the title of "peacemaker."

One has to view Catherine's activities in the light of her own age. During the Middle Ages women were romanticized, made the idols of song and poetry, courted by lovers in elaborate ways, but really not meaning very much. They were the daughters of their families, then the wives of their husbands, and then the mothers of their sons and daughters, and then the grieving widows. Such widows, because they were older and experienced, were allowed considerable freedom and had a certain limited power in anything to do with family and social affairs. The power was allowed because the women had survived to ripe old ages, something rare in that period.

After a particularly nasty confrontation brought about by jealous Tertiaries, Catherine was provided with a new spiritual director and confessor, Blessed Raymond of Capua. He was a well-educated man who would become the head of the Dominicans eventually. He would also be the main biographer of Catherine's life, the author of the central source of information about her. It must be remembered that Catherine of Siena did not know how to read or write when she grew up. She dictated her works to her educated friends, who wrote down what she told them.

In the summer of 1370, Catherine received a remarkable vision and the command to heal the wounds of the faithful around her. At that time the city of Florence was feuding with the pope, Gregory XI, who lived not in Rome, the traditional home of the pontiffs (or popes), but in the French city of Avignon. Gregory was there because for many decades the pontiffs had lived in France, under the stern influence of the French kings who enjoyed having a kind of control over the papacy. The kings feared allowing the popes to return to Rome, of course, and so this caused many difficulties for the Holy Father back in Italy.

One source of the trouble for the popes was the great cities, such as Florence, that rebelled against papal authority whenever a difference of opinion arose. Pope Gregory used powerful spiritual punishments to make sure that people followed the truth, such as the one depriving the entire city of all of the sacraments. To make peace, the Florentines sent a delegation to Catherine asking for help in sending an olive branch to the pope.

Now Catherine knew about the pitiful state of Rome, abandoned by the popes. Riots took place in the streets of the Eternal City, many were starving and without jobs because the economy was so poor, cattle grazed around some of the finest churches in the world because grass was growing there, and nobles and troublemakers plotted against one another and against the pope to make sure he never returned and end their scheming. Worst of all, Catherine realized that the spiritual life of the city was suffering. Because Rome was the heart of the Church — that is, the see, or seat of the bishop, founded by Saint Peter himself — the whole Church suffered by the absence of Peter's descendants, the representatives of Christ on earth.

Determined to do what she could, Catherine accepted the people of Florence's request to represent them before the pope. She hoped, however, to do much more that just make peace between Gregory and the Florentines. She planned to convince the pope to go back to Rome. Fortunately, she already knew Gregory. They had sent each other letters, and the Holy Father respected her greatly. Sadly, he refused to do anything about Florence (peace would be made under a later pope), but he was disposed to hear her words about Rome.

Catherine prayed and was given an important secret: She was told that Pope Gregory had secretly made a vow to return one day to the Eternal City, as Rome was always called. He hesitated, however, because of the troubles he would have to face in going back and because of the constant refusal of the French king and the French cardinals even to consider such an idea. Catherine went before the pope courageously and told him his innermost secret. He admitted that she was right and resolved (or promised) to return to Rome, where he had to bring needed reforms to the Church, and to raise the faith to new heights of glory.

From the start Gregory was opposed by the French, who were horrified at the news of what the pope planned to do, throwing fits or fainting in shock. Rather than trying to convince the pope not to go, the French cardinals figured to weaken the pope's plans by attacking Catherine of Siena. They insisted on putting her on trial for heresy and assorted crimes, using the false and cruel rumors that were spread by her enemies and even repeated by the French themselves. They calculated that if they could condemn Catherine, the pope would forget about going back to Rome, because he had been duped by a fraud or a witch.

Catherine, however, was able to overcome their charges and accusations. Each attack upon her was defeated with simple, devout honesty, and with such obvious goodness that the three bishops who were in charge of the trial sat taken aback. They declared her free of all possible stain. The French were defeated, and to their frustration, the pope was even more set on going back to Rome.

Overcoming all objections, Gregory departed Avignon on September 13, 1376, traveling slowly to the Eternal City. There was a glorious parade and celebrations in the city when he entered, but the joy was soon reduced by the same squabbling and unrest in the streets. Troubles plagued the pontiff from the start, and, under terrible stress, he died. During the reign of the pope who would follow him, Urban VI, the Church would enter into one of its most difficult times, and Catherine would have a part to play in those events as well.

Catherine, meanwhile, faced her own challenges. On the fourth Sunday of Lent in 1375, while in Pisa, she was given the stigmata, a very special gift from God. The stigmata is the name given to the wounds similar to those suffered by the crucified Christ that appear on individuals chosen by God. Extremely rare, the stigmata has been given to only a few people in history, including Saint Francis of Assisi and Padre Pio. They had the stigmata in its traditional form, meaning that the wounds were visible to the eye, even bleeding. Catherine received the stigmata in a different way. Wise to the ways of her fellow humans, she prayed that the signs would be hidden on her flesh until her death. She knew how eagerly people would flock around her if she carried visible signs of Christ's passion.

They would not come out of faith but curiosity. Such thrill-seekers would only complicate her life and make enemies for her everywhere. If she had a mission, she needed a certain amount of peace in order to work God's will. The signs were not visible until her death, but they were there, nevertheless. She bore the painful wounds on her hands and on her feet, and had pain in her heart, which had also been pierced.

Catherine spent some time bringing Siena a revitalized faith, and she served as a special ambassador for the Holy Father. As a further aid in her mission, Catherine miraculously learned how to read and to write. This was of enormous value because many of the powerful looked down on her, dismissing her with scorn because she could not read, an important symbol of the learned. Catherine still preferred to dictate her thoughts to secretaries whenever possible, to save time, being a very practical woman about using her resources. She dictated her most famous work, *Dialogue*, a volume of meditations and divine revelations given to her by God.

In the meantime, Pope Urban VI in Rome had begun his reign as head of the Church with plans for many reforms. The pontiff, unfortunately, was quite eccentric and heavy-handed. A severe person, he offended many cardinals with his demands and arbitrary methods — meaning he often did not explain himself, and what he commanded often made little sense. Many of these cardinals grew so upset that they rebelled against the pope, electing their own man in his place. The person they chose, with the encouragement of the French, was named Robert of Geneva. He took the name Pope Clement VII, but he was hardly a real pope. Instead, he is called by history an antipope, a rival to the legitimate pope.

From time to time in the past, certain men have been named antipopes against the true successor of Peter. Such men have claimed to be the genuine pontiff, but they owed their title not to the right and proper election by the cardinals but by the backing of some king or emperor who hoped to weaken the real pope or take control of the Holy See, as the papacy is also called.

The election of Antipope Clement was the start of what has been called the Great Schism or Great Western Schism, a period from 1378 until 1417 when the Church was divided into different camps, with one side favoring the true pontiff and another supporting the antipope. At one point during the long and difficult years that were to follow, there would, at one point, be three different papal claimants: the true pope and two antipopes.

From the start, Catherine realized what the division of the Church would mean. It would be a disaster. While Urban had many faults, he was the rightful successor to Saint Peter. That was all Catherine needed to know. She declared Clement — who had taken up residence in Avignon — to be an enemy and a false pontiff.

Pope Urban summoned Catherine to Rome in November 1378. He asked her aid and support in his cause, which she immediately embraced. She moved to Rome from Siena and began writing to everyone she knew pleading for their help to aid the Holy Father. It is useful to remember that she counted among her friends, her "children," a number of kings, queens, nobles, high Church leaders, and powerful merchants. Her letters were as eloquent as ever, but Urban had made many enemies and, at the time, it seemed that

Antipope Clement might find enough support to topple Urban from the papal throne. Her friends were reluctant to join in her fight, perhaps waiting to see how events would turn out. They could not afford, they thought, to choose the wrong person in a fight as important as the future of the Church.

The struggle for the Chair of Saint Peter had scattered the faithful in all directions. Catherine knew that Pope Urban was the leader given to the Church by God. He could be quite frustrating and stubborn, but that would not alter (or change) God's will. Truth is the truth, she explained. These words fell largely on deaf ears. Her "children" lacked her trust in God and her faith in what was right.

This is a totally human response, as weak, cowardly, and illogical as it seems. Even today, when people recognize lies or evil, they are paralyzed and afraid. They advise everyone to "look at the situation from both sides" or caution others "not to judge." Such people play it safe, going against their own consciences and what they know to be right; and because of their fears, hesitations, and cowardice, evil is permitted to prosper, while the holy souls can only mourn and pray.

Catherine, bent on ending the schism, was using up the last of her strength. Growing weaker, she was eventually confined to her bed. Even there she managed to aid the papacy. She reconciled Pope Urban VI with the local Roman government, called the Commune, in 1380. This permitted the popes to stay in Rome over the following years without fear of being driven from the city or of having their capitol, the place from which they were struggling to overcome their enemies, sink into chaos or war.

These successes were Catherine's last acts. On April 21, 1380, she suffered a severe stroke that left her paralyzed. A little over a week later, on April 29, she died.

On her deathbed the stigmata, which she had carried for many years, finally appeared before the astonished eyes of her friends. She was well beyond the curiosity or envy of her fellow human beings. Her life had been spent following her simple rule. She believed that all people — whether in the monastery or the world — have to develop a basic self-knowledge; they must keep trying to become new and better individuals each and every day. Self-knowledge means recognizing failures, weaknesses, and sins. Whether God seems near or far, the soul must give praise and fulfill all of the tasks set before it as God's will.

She lived on a level of prayer that few human beings know of, let alone understand. She had gone through an "espousal," a marriage with Christ, that had become the focus of all her energies. It did not matter where she was or what she was doing. Christ was the total purpose of her life, which lasted the same number of years as that of her Divine Spouse, thirty-three.

Catherine of Siena was canonized in 1461. She was named patroness of Italy in 1939, and Pope Paul VI declared her a Doctor of the Church in 1970. Saint Catherine's feast day is April 29.

Chapter 4

Crispina

Everyone in the world has a relative very much like the great martyr Saint Crispina, or at least everyone can remember such an individual in the family long ago. She may have been called Agatha, Grace, Catherine, or Hattie; but her resemblance to the historical Crispina is uncanny in many cases. Such an aunt, cousin, or in-law is or was a no-nonsense type of person, sometimes described as "crusty but benign."

In other words, this is a human being who views all things quite clearly — firmly set in black and white, with no middle ground and no wishy-washy attitudes to confuse situations. There are no fuzzy gray areas where people or events are concerned, no doubts or misgivings. For the Crispinas of the world right is right, wrong is wrong, and everything in between is just so much hogwash. These women have well-trained, firm moral values that set the patterns of their lives, and they expect others to have some level of understanding about what is expected from a normal, sane human being in God's presence.

It seems as if people today are being raised without the necessary moral values that would enable them to function as truly rational beings. They grow up unsure about right and wrong, afraid to make a judgment about any issue and easily swayed by catchy slogans used to sell everything from soap to political campaigns. In fact, people today are suddenly discovering to their shock and dismay that the virtues and beauty of ages past are fading away while they sit dumbstruck and confused about genuine morality. The Crispinas of the world thus stand apart and alone, but by their presence they show everyone else the insanity of "going along to get along" in a mad society.

The original Crispina lived in the third and fourth centuries A.D., having the bad luck of being around while Diocletian sat upon the imperial throne of Rome, from 284 to 305. As Roman emperors go,

Diocletian was not half bad, at least in the earlier years of his reign. His name is associated, however, with the last and most ghastly Christian persecutions, when the blood of martyrs flowed freely throughout the entire Roman world.

Some historians point to Diocletian's early years, when his tolerant approach to Christianity allowed it to flourish everywhere. These historians claim that Diocletian's co-emperor (called an Augustus), a man named Galerius, urged him to start the persecutions in order to halt Christianity's spread. Even the nobles of the Roman Empire were converting, Galerius probably argued, and these individuals were the main support of the throne. If everyone accepted the Christian idea of equality before God, Rome would be destroyed and the emperor sent packing over the next hill without so much as a fare-thee-well from the people.

Whatever the arguments and whoever made them, Diocletian took note and decided to embark on a full-scale era of anti-Christian policies. He probably was afraid of the logical outcome of the Christian principles and declared that imperial officials were "to tear down the churches to the foundations, and to destroy the Sacred Scriptures by fire . . . and that those in honorable stations should be degraded if they persevered in their adherence to Christianity." Obviously this emperor was a man who carried a decision to the farthest extreme once he had made his mind up about a matter. Three more edicts issued by Diocletian, probably to strengthen his political hand, resulted in imprisonment of bishops and Church leaders, the torture of laypeople, and eventually the martyrdom of many true believers.

Now the fury and the scale of local persecutions depended very much upon the personalities and the enthusiasm of local governors and their aides. In some areas the officials took to persecuting Christians like ducks take to water. In other regions the officials made an effort to maintain a sense of dignity and decorum, while eliminating a large portion of the population in a sensible, methodical way.

One such official was the proconsul Anulinus, who handled Roman affairs in the city of Thagara, in Africa. Many powerful Roman families lived in the province, and Anulinus had to watch himself very carefully, because some of these aristocrats had ties to the imperial court. He had to appear as enthusiastic as the next man about burning and beating women and children if he planned to keep his position. Crispina, however, presented him with a genuine problem. She belonged to an exalted rank of Romans in Thagara, being an older matron, married, and the mother of children. As a result, Anulinus had to watch his step in her case. She had to die, and everyone knew that, but he had to make the trial look compassionate, just, and legal.

During the persecutions, on December 5, 304, the Roman matron Crispina was brought before Anulinus and charged with the crime of being a Christian. The Romans standing around probably gasped and pretended shock and alarm when they heard the accusations against her. It was considered smart to pretend to be surprised when the word Christian came up in trials or even in conversations. No one wanted to have the label of Christian-lover attached to his or her name. That could bring about all sorts of terrible reactions from friends and family, and it might even bring one to the attention of a Roman magistrate.

Crispina was very precise in her response before the court when she heard the charges leveled against her, followed by the necessary shock and alarm from her friends and neighbors. She said she was a Christian and would remain so until her death. When the court demanded that she sacrifice to the traditional gods of Rome, an act that displayed the court's compassionate and just manner, Crispina announced in a loud and clear voice that there was only one God. She certainly had better things to do than throw pinches of incense or salt on idols that were just pieces of wood and stone. It was an insult for anyone to ask her to put her mind on hold just to save her life.

Anulinus was horrified, of course, because Crispina was a model of the Roman matron, an example of all that the Romans held dear. Seeing her before him, so sure and so set in her faith, made him afraid because in her precise words she was raising Christianity to an entirely different level as a religion. Romans prided themselves on logic, clear thinking, and courage; and Christianity, according to this matron, demanded the same things.

To make matters worse, this was no uneducated slave slobbering about a heaven that would offer rewards to just anybody. This was a no-nonsense aristocratic Roman matron carefully explaining that Christianity was the only course open to anyone with a brain.

The proconsul was beside himself at the sight of her and decided on a way to make Crispina lose her standing before the crowds. He ordered his men to hold her down and to shave her head in public. Roman matrons, it seems, were very proud of their long tresses, and they wore elaborate braids, pompadours, and ringlets as part of the changing styles over the centuries. Crispina was deprived of her crown of radiant beauty. She stood before her fellow Romans starkly bald as a result of the punishment handed down by Anulinus.

Even that did not reduce the impact of her declarations. If the proconsul hoped to make her an object of mockery, he failed. Crispina's children wept at the sight of her, but they could not persuade her to sacrifice to pagan gods who no longer commanded her respect or loyalty. Right was right, and Crispina was determined to stand by her conversion to the truth, no matter what Anulinus or his henchmen did to her.

In the end, of course, there was only one possible verdict, the only one in keeping with the emperor's decrees. Crispina was condemned to death. She did not flinch, did not cry for mercy but thanked God for having been shown the Light of Christ. Crispina gracefully bowed and offered her shaved head to the executioner. She died with joy, the same sort of exultation seen in the faces of Christian martyrs throughout the empire.

The Acts of the Martyrdom of Saint Crispina were written a short time after her death in 304. Diocletian lived only one year longer than she did, but the persecutions of the Christians continued another seven years after her burial.

December 5 was celebrated as Saint Crispina's feast day when the great Saint Augustine was alive and preaching to the faithful of the Church. His brilliant mind, reflecting the onetime honor and intellectual abilities of the Roman people, appreciated the no-nonsense approach of Crispina, and he spoke of her often in his sermons. On December 5 the Church still honors this remarkable Roman matron.

Chapter 5

Denis

The beautiful, modern City of Lights and Lovers — Paris — was once called Lutetia and was part of the sprawling Roman Empire, in the province called Gaul by the Romans and what is today France. The present name, conjuring up images of charm and romance, was taken from a local tribe called the Parisis, who happened to live in the area when the Romans marched in with their legions. The Romans subjected the Parisis to all the doubtful benefits of what passed then as civilization and then fought hordes of wild barbarians in order to control Lutetia, perhaps realizing or simply hoping that one day it would become an important world city.

Paris, or Lutetia, was lovely, but it was not immune to the political and religious upheavals of the empire — a fact of life faced by the millions of men, women, and children who formed the Roman domain. Thus when the Roman emperor Decius (ruling from 249 to 251) began his terrible persecutions of the Christian Church, the city suffered really shocking losses, as the faith was secure there and Christians went to their deaths rather than betray the Savior. Such devout Christians were martyred by the Romans with their usual organized methods, while the cowardly worshiped any Roman god put in front of their noses in order to stay alive. This sort of wholesale death and betrayal resulted in fear and chaos, and the Church in Paris was broken and rendered ineffectual, which was Decius' intent, after all.

This emperor was a man who greatly feared the Church, and he is quoted by historians of the time as announcing: "I would rather hear of a usurper [in this instance, someone who takes over the Roman throne] with five legions of soldiers at his command than learn another Bishop of Rome had been chosen."

The Bishop of Rome (another name for the Holy Father) at the time was Pope Fabian, who sat in the Chair of Peter from 236 to 250. Fabian understood Decius and his brutal methods against the Church, cruelties that had torn apart the Christian society in Paris with a terrible efficiency. Something had to be done, therefore, despite the obvious dangers, to restore the fold and to make the Church secure again. The pontiff's response to the destruction that had taken place in Paris and to the spiritual upheaval brought about by imperial command was a young man named Denis.

Saint Denis, now the patron of France, was bishop of Paris, and his spirit has inspired generations of French people over the turbulent centuries since his death. Most historians believe that Denis was born somewhere in Italy, but little is known of his early life or education. Actually, scholars have been arguing about Saint Denis for so long that no one is sure about anything except for the fact that he was in Paris and served the Parisian people before he was martyred. Because he was an energetic builder, Denis (or Dionysius, as he is also known) left a remarkable legacy of stone witnesses to his mission in the City of Lights.

He was chosen by Pope Fabian because he was healthy, rational, and virtuous — a winning combination in any era. He was also an ordained priest who was well trained in spiritual matters, which certainly added to his qualifications. He could be counted on to persevere with prudence and with the grace of God. He also had the physical stamina that allowed him to make the journey into France, then called Gaul, and to adjust to life there among strangers. He was provided with letters of authority from the pope and two companions (Rusticus, an ordained priest, and a deacon named Eleutherius).

Arriving in Paris, which was even then a sprawling trade center, Denis and his companions were welcomed by the remaining Christians who were thrilled to know that the Holy Father in Rome knew about their sufferings. Denis established his headquarters right away, choosing a spot on an island in the Seine River. That beautiful river meanders through the City of Lights even today, reflecting the soaring splendor of Notre Dame Cathedral in its dark currents. On the river island, Denis erected a chapel and started regular religious services for the Parisians. The establishment of the new chapel caused an instant stir, and countless numbers of worshipers attended services held there.

Denis also built a crypt chapel dedicated to the Blessed Virgin

Mary on a site that eventually became the Monastery of Notre-Dame-des-Champs. Near the modern Notre Dame Cathedral, the saintly bishop erected a chapel called in the days after his death St. Denis-du-Pas. Tradition states that Denis and his companions were tried by the local Roman officials on that spot, and it became a popular destination for French pilgrims. By the seventh century a basilica covered Denis's grave, as his veneration was always part of the Parisian spiritual life.

As the Christians of Paris rejoiced over the new houses of worship established by Denis, others in Paris were viewing the bishop's efforts with growing anger and dismay. These were the heathen priests and leaders of the area, those still worshiping the old gods of blood and sacrifice, of barbarism and war. The Romans allowed such pagan practices to continue unmolested, reserving their persecutions for the Christians, who were seen as the real threat to the empire.

The priests of the old gods watched Denis gathering new converts every day, and they saw their power and prestige falling as rapidly. Who would listen to their rantings about the old gods when splendid new churches were rising throughout the city, calling the people to Christ? Denis had an instinct for beauty, and all of his chapels and parish structures offered not only the Word of Christ but harmony of stone and shadows, unique havens for the sense of order that rests in all human beings. The pagans knew that these new buildings offered a rebirth of sorts, something they could not match or defeat with their old, bloodied altars and thatched gathering places. The pagan priests fumed for a time, and then they decided to meet together to handle the crisis of Denis's presence with a united front. They started their campaigns by preaching against the Christians and inciting riots. People in all historical periods use riots as weapons against one another, and in Denis's time the local pagans had the riot down to an art form. They could gather mobs to burn and pillage, kill and loot with real enthusiasm, and then afterward everyone went to their local pagan shrine for a feast of celebration.

The riots proved highly ineffective because Paris was entering a new age, one that the pagan priests and their followers did not understand at the moment. Riots have to be well timed in order to succeed, and it became increasingly obvious that the Parisians were tired of the same old race through the streets to bring death and terror. The pagans had a perfectly marvelous time destroying sections of the city in their rage, but they could not lure anyone else to join them, and that took half the fun out of the display.

Now this defeat proved costly to the pagan priests, who had to sit down with one another again to come up with a new solution, one that took changes and different points of view into consideration. The priests probably came up with all sorts of grand ideas about new riots, even more ferocious than the last; but then they settled on the only solution possible for them, one their ancestors had used for decades. The pagans went to the Roman governor, Fescennius Sisinnius, demanding that he follow Roman custom by putting an end to Denis and to the revival of the Christian community of Paris. It was really just that simple, and the pagans probably kicked themselves for wasting so much time marching through the streets.

As a result of the pagan plea, naturally, the governor began to investigate Denis and his companions. Lapsed Christians, those who had turned their back on Christ to escape martyrdom, were only too happy to provide evidence about the work of the Christian bishop and his aides. If they didn't have anything real or substantial, they made up stuff or hinted at really wicked plots and programs. The saint and his companions were arrested sometime in the year 275, although some records claim this happened as early as 258.

Dragged before a Roman court and faced with the traditional command to deny Christ or die, Saints Denis, Rusticus, and Eleutherius refused to make any such cowardly gesture. They were badly beaten as a result and returned to the court. When they still refused to deny the faith, the three were put on the rack, mauled by wild beasts, burned, and then beheaded. These various methods of trying to make them change their mind seem a bit excessive. The Romans must have been hard put to break Denis. Maybe the Roman executioners and torturers were having a bad day and liked to try their hand at new ways of seeing people die. They certainly accomplished their orders. Denis was no more.

If the pagans in the area thought they had won the battle by having the saint's head chopped off, they were in for a rude awakening. To begin with, Denis refused to be disposed of in the time-honored Roman manner. His body and those of his companions were thrown into the Seine by the executioners as a matter of course. Denis's corpse, however, did not sink into the murky depths; rather, it astonished many by rising to the surface and carrying its severed head in its arms. Portraits of Denis depict him as holding his head in his hands because of this event. It is a rather grim but effective way of announcing how he died for Christ. The three bodies were removed from their watery grave because of the courage of a Parisian matron named Catulla. She and her friends saw the body rise and dared to follow its course along the river, saving the remains when they came to rest and giving them Christian burial.

Secondly, in death Denis had even more influence over the people of France. The pagan priests who demanded the murder died unknown, forgotten, and lost to the memory of even their own kind. Denis was never lost to the hearts and minds of the people he had served, and they bequeathed a holy tradition to the generations that followed his death.

Over the centuries a Parisian holy custom developed, called the Seven Stations of Saint Denis. Each of these stations — designated sites that were known to have been a part of the saint's apostolate and martyrdom — was visited in the annual celebrations held in Paris. The Seven Stations of Saint Denis were popular until the French Revolution, when so many of the historical religious structures were destroyed by crazed rioters.

Saint Denis's feast day is October 9, and throughout France, especially in the lovely City of Lights, he continues to renew the Church and inspire new generations of the faithful.

Dominic Savio

Chapter 6

Dominic Savio

One thing that has become very rare in the modern world is pure goodness. When faced with the ever-glowing beauty of goodness in a single human being, other people feel nostalgia — a longing for the "good old days" when the world was a kinder place and everyone was innocent about many evils.

Holiness reminds human beings of heaven itself and of the time in their lives when they were not lazy, not quick to judge or gossip, not yet exposed to modern civilization's lusts and desires. Growing up on mean streets or in a media-filled environment changes most men and women. As Pope Pius XII declared: "You are what you take into your mind and heart though your senses." That means that all the TV images, the films, the magazines, and the words spoken to an individual can alter the way he or she sees life. The filth and ugliness so evident in today's world cling to small minds, dirtying them and making them vulnerable to evil. Because of the seemingly countless instances of such crudeness and immorality that are seen everywhere today, few humans can look back on their lives and know that they kept their souls spotless.

The world and its temptations rush in upon the young, corrupting their values, making them want things that have no real place in the life of a Christian. Because this process has gone on throughout history — slower in most centuries because there were no TV's or movies or magazines — most of the Friends of God, the saints, had to take a stand at some point against the world, temptations, and their own desires. Such men and women, realizing how insane it is to want pleasures and passions that fade and die, repent and begin to restore the balance of their lives, becoming holy. This act of repentance and this day-by-day self-discipline and change are all part and parcel of becoming a saint.

That particular process, of course, was not necessary for Saint Dominic Savio. The motto that he adopted at the age of five or six, and the one that has (or should have) deep meaning for all people living in our modern era, was "Death but not sin."

Dominic Savio was born on April 2, 1842, in Riva di Chieri in northern Italy. He came from a peasant family: hardworking, decent people who lived close to the land and kept the faith in their daily routines. The child was unusual from the start, aware of many things that most children ignore until they are older. He radiated holiness and sat still and was interested in church even as a toddler.

Neighbors and the local parish priest were as dumbfounded as Dominic's parents were by the fact that the little boy displayed a unique ability to read people's hearts and minds. He would sit, solemnly staring at a man or woman, and the grownup would realize that his or her innermost secrets were coming to light. Dominic could also predict the future, sometimes telling people things to avoid or events that would take place.

Now usually the presence of such a saintly, supernaturally gifted person drives friends and neighbors wild. They are afraid of things they do not understand or wonder how a child could come to possess these strange gifts. It seems, however, that this did not occur in the case of Dominic Savio. He was so small, so happy, so handsome, that everyone in the town believed that they were blessed by his presence. It was like having a tiny archangel in residence.

Dominic grew up in the close-knit world of a peasant community, attending school and church with his friends and classmates. One of these would later testify: "As long as Dominic was with us, not one of us dared to say a bad word." Dominic, in turn, was also aware of the fact that he was different. He confided once: "God wants me to become a saint. If I don't, I shall be a failure."

At the age of seven, Dominic received his First Communion and served as an altar boy in his parish church. His parish priest was impressed by the child, not only because of Dominic's purity and holiness, but because the lad was bright and eager to learn. The priest kept watch on the boy and then introduced him to a visitor, Saint John Bosco (or Don Bosco, as he was popularly known), who had come into the region from his headquarters in Turin, Italy.

One of Don Bosco's missions in the world was to educate young men who were too poor to enter the institutions of higher levels on their own. Dominic's parish priest was well aware of the lad's qualifications, and he knew that the family could not afford to educate him properly. Dominic was therefore interviewed by Don Bosco, who said: "I was quite surprised to see the wonderful workings of divine grace in a boy so young."

At the age of twelve, Dominic went to Turin to study at Saint John Bosco's school. He was being prepared for the seminary, but he knew that he would never see the priesthood. Dominic understood that his time on earth would be brief. For this reason he was aware of the vital aspect of life called "now."

For too many humans, life becomes a dream, a hope for the future that never quite turns out properly. These individuals spend so much time dreaming about tomorrow that they never live each "today." In other words, they do not understand that each day of life is given to them to accomplish the tasks at home, to gain strength and resolve, and to move slowly toward all the coming tomorrows. Most importantly, such men and women forget a simple fact of human life: Yesterday is past and lost; tomorrow may never come; therefore, today is the only important thing, the only guaranteed period of twenty-four hours in which all of one's dreams and hopes can be made possible.

Saint Dominic Savio, knowing that he did not have that many tomorrows, sought holiness in each single day. He perfected this approach to life by consecrating himself to the Blessed Virgin Mary at the age of twelve. He also asked Saint John Bosco if he could fast and do penance.

Don Bosco, wise in the spiritual life and aware of the physical stamina of twelve-year-olds, denied Dominic the right to do anything harsh or strenuous. Instead, he cautioned: "The penance God asks is obedience. Do the penance of daily bearing with injuries, suffering, cold, heat, tiredness. . . ."

Dominic's spiritual gifts were well known to Don Bosco, who led the child carefully. In some cases a prophecy or vision given to Dominic was confided to those involved. It is believed that Pope Pius IX heard one such vision experienced by Dominic. As a result of this extraordinary grace, the Holy Father restored the Catholic hierarchy (meaning all of the bishops) to England in 1850. The Church had not been represented by prelates (the name used for bishops and Church leaders) since the time of King Henry VIII in the 1500s.

In the school, Dominic formed a special group, the Company of the Immaculate Conception, designed to take tough young kids and transform their characters. Because of Dominic's winning ways, he attracted many members and greatly aided the work of Don Bosco. Dominic taught catechism classes, visited the sick, and kept peace in the dormitories. Each day he seemed to grow more beautiful, filled with a holy light and a peace that shone upon his classmates.

Then, in 1856, when Dominic was only fourteen, he became very ill. Don Bosco and the school staff tried to restore him to health, but it became clear quickly that the sickness would take its toll. The illness was sapping his strength and his life. After talking about it with his parents, it was decided that Dominic would have to leave the school, to return to his family.

The parting of Saint John Bosco and Saint Dominic Savio was an emotional one, as they knew that they would never see one another again in this life. Because of their sanctity and their beliefs, however, the parting would be only temporary, only in the physical sense. Time and distance do not matter to those who are united in Christ. All people part from those they love and respect. These two saints had been allowed each other's company for three years, sharing many joyous hours in which they were able to open their hearts to speak freely of their spiritual lives. Many saints have no such consolations on earth. They know wondrous secrets, overflow with joy, but they keep such things to themselves usually because they are surrounded by other humans who think only in the world's terms. Dominic and Don Bosco had known one another, however briefly. Now they could go on with their individual missions, having been blessed with each other's presence.

Dominic's family received their ill child with both joy and sorrow. They were thrilled to have the lad safely home again, but a chill must have come upon them when they realized his physical condition. (The family is reported as living in Mondonio, Italy, at the time.)

Cared for and watched over, Dominic remained at home, receiving visits from friends and neighbors. His prayer life was becoming more and more constant and his physical strength continued to fade. While others blinked backed their tears, Dominic smiled and comforted them.

On March 9, 1857, he asked his father to send for the parish priest. It was time for the last rites, or the sacrament of the anointing of the sick, by which Holy Mother Church continues her role of counseling and guiding souls through the brief span of time known as a human's life. Dominic received the Viaticum, as the sacrament was called in Latin, and then he returned to his prayers.

Later that evening he asked his father to help him recite the prayer for a happy death. Then he cried out: "Oh, Dad, what a beautiful sight I see!" Dominic Savio had obviously seen a glimpse of Paradise, or heaven, just as he died.

He was beatified (that is, named Blessed) in 1950. Four years later he was canonized, thus becoming one of the youngest lads ever raised to the altars of the Church who was not a martyr. Saint Dominic's feast day is March 9.

Elizabeth of Portugal

Chapter 7

Elizabeth of Portugal

Some men and women become saints just by living with their nutty relatives. Their lives are marred by one family feud after another, and they spend their days coping with vain, unreasonable, and sometimes really stupid relations who believe that they are the true centers of the universe and the only persons in the world who have sufferings or trials. Saint Elizabeth of Portugal was just such an individual, and she earned the title of "the Peacemaker" because of what she endured at the hands of family members, some of whom were really strange.

She was born in 1271, the royal daughter of King Pedro III and Queen Constantia of Aragon, in Spain. Named after her great aunt, Saint Elizabeth of Hungary, and raised in a pious manner, she was taught to recite the Divine Office (the prayers recited throughout the day and night in monasteries). This did not leave much time for childish amusements, of course, but in those days children of royal blood were raised to fulfill their obligations without complaints. Elizabeth, like others of the royal families of Europe, learned from the cradle that obligations were all that they possessed in the world.

Her childhood was rather brief, anyway, as she was married at the age of twelve to King Diniz (Denis) of Portugal, who was called *Re Laurador*, the "Working King," because of his labors for the nation. Diniz was a poet as well as a king, and he was known as having no morals whatsoever, which must have come as a shock to Elizabeth, his pious bride. He carried on affairs with all sorts of women and allowed his courtiers to live in the vilest states of evil and corruption, a fact of life that was not very pleasant for a Spanish twelve-year-old who had been sent to make the court a Christian paradise.

She, in turn, startled the courtiers of King Diniz because of her

loveliness, her royal elegance, and her meek and gentle ways. The
courtiers could not believe their eyes when she appeared in their
midst. The last thing they needed was a pious, kind, and long-
suffering young woman at the king's side. If she gained influence over
the king, the party was over for most of the hangers-on in the court,
and knowing this they began to hunt for ways in which they could
make Elizabeth too weak to count against them.

They tried tempting her with various pleasures and sinful ways,
telling her of their love for her, bringing expensive gifts and offering
her wines and ales in order to get her too drunk to know her own
mind. Elizabeth remained steadfastly distant and pure, having been
trained in her parents' home to know about such things and the ways
in which to avoid them. She was saintly, but she was not stupid. Upset
by these failures, the courtiers decided to smear the young queen's
reputation instead. Dirty gossip can always be a weapon against an
enemy, because people delight in believing all the worst things about
their friends, especially those in high places.

One particularly evil page began a whispering campaign about
Elizabeth and a young man in the palace. The gossip reached Diniz's
ears eventually, and he condemned the young man to death without a
trial. That resulted in an episode that shocked the entire court and
brought about the conversion of many of the king's closest allies,
prompted solely by terror.

Somehow, and no one has ever been able to give a reasonable
explanation for the truly horrendous happening, the young man
condemned to a hideous and prolonged death never was taken to the
place of execution. The one arrested by accident was the evil page,
who screamed and cried as he underwent the various forms of torture
intended for an innocent victim of the page's own plot. When news of
the mistaken identity and the accidental execution swept through the
palace, the page's allies fainted, fled, or made their confessions,
depending upon how alarmed they became.

The king received official word of the long, drawn-out
execution, and when the victim's name was announced he almost had
a stroke. He was not stupid either, and he had an understanding of
divine retribution, a fact that forced him to discuss the matter with his
wife. It did not take long for Diniz to realize that the page had lied to
him and had plotted the downfall of Elizabeth and the death of an
innocent young man. After that remarkable incident and the revealed

truth of the matters, Diniz softened in his attitude toward Elizabeth because it was obviously too dangerous to be her enemy.

What Elizabeth thought about the wretched event was never recorded. As a royal woman, she had learned early to keep her secrets and opinions to herself. Few of the courtiers were evil enough to try what the page had tried in vain, but the queen learned to keep her own counsel and to rely solely upon God.

Because Diniz was busy with governing or with his nightly parties, Elizabeth was able to spend her time in prayer and in the service of the needy. The political system of the period and the lack of even basic hygiene resulted in thousands of poor people dying and in thousands more becoming victims of disease. Like her namesake, Elizabeth of Hungary, the queen felt compassion and concern for all who were suffering, and she spent a great deal of her time starting institutions and organizations that would ease the plight of the people.

She bore two children to Diniz: Alfonso IV, who would succeed Diniz on the throne of Portugal, and a daughter, Constantia. King Diniz had fathered all sorts of illegitimate children over the years as well, and he paraded them before the court and rewarded their mothers with titles and lands. Such daily demonstrations of past infidelities, and the introduction of Diniz's new mistresses were not pleasant events for Elizabeth to endure under the watchful eyes of the court. She was kind to the illegitimate children and avoided encounters with the mistresses, who were sometimes ambitious and strangely proud of their affairs. Diniz spent time with such women, allowing Elizabeth to continue her own spiritual exercises and her charitable works. Elizabeth founded convents, hospitals, and shelters during this period of her life.

As the years passed, however, the young heir, Alfonso, grew bitter over his father's immorality and contact with his illegitimate offspring. Certainly Diniz did seem to favor the sons and daughters of his mistresses, and such children were with him each day, while Alfonso was kept at a distance. He grew up in Elizabeth's care, angry at his father and eager to begin his own reign, a time in which he hoped to restore the monarchy to a moral awareness.

Alfonso rebelled against his father on two separate occasions, going so far as to raise an army and engaging Diniz in battle. Elizabeth, caught between her husband and son, worked to make peace. Diniz blamed her for one of Alfonso's rebellions and threw her out of the palace. When Elizabeth continued to travel between the king and Alfonso, however, Diniz relented. He realized that she favored no one but was only trying to stop the bloodshed. Elizabeth returned to the palace to discover that Diniz had learned the truth about many aspects of his life.

Elizabeth's kindness, gentleness, and ability to endure the scorn of the king's mistresses won him over. He was probably aware of death approaching, a knowledge that brings about spiritual recovery in all kinds of human beings in time. His wayward lifestyle did not aid the throne or the nation. His abuse of his wife and heir reflected badly upon him and his noble line. Diniz sent his mistresses and their children packing and settled down with Elizabeth to face his remaining years with Christian dignity.

When he died in 1325, Elizabeth was at his side, and he had been reconciled with the Church and the sacraments. Alfonso IV was crowned the new ruler of Portugal and installed with his family in Diniz's place. That event, of course, opened the way for Elizabeth as she sought a new life.

Playing the role of queen dowager, or queen mother, is never easy, especially when the new king is as independent and fiery-tempered as Alfonso was in his own right. Elizabeth saw him safely in control of the country and then announced that it was time for her to retire from court life.

She bid farewell to one and all in the palace and traveled with an escort to the city of Coimbra, to the Convent of the Poor Clares. There she entered the cloister and put aside her splendid gowns to wear the brown robes of the Franciscan Tertiaries, the Third Order founded by Saint Francis of Assisi. Although she had lived all of her life as a truly religious soul, Elizabeth was now able to spend her days and nights in the silence of the convent. The Divine Office that she had recited each day since her childhood was now sung in the convent choir. She was "home," able to be "alone with The Alone."

Her peace was shattered, however, in 1336, when Alfonso announced that he was going to war against Ferdinand of Castile. Alfonso's daughter, Maria, had been married to Ferdinand and had written a pathetic plea for aid. Her husband, it appears, did not like her very much and was abusing her rather severely. As a father, and as a son who had witnessed such treatment visited upon his mother over the years, Alfonso was in a rage.

Hearing the news, Elizabeth left the convent and traveled to Estremoz, where the two armies were facing each other. The sight of Elizabeth and her escort arriving on the battlefield brought the war preparations to a halt, and she was able to summon both Ferdinand and Alfonso to a conference. It took hours of furious debate and occasional outbursts of anger, but Elizabeth was able to bring about a series of compromises that avoided a catastrophic war and yet provided her granddaughter, Maria, with guarantees of safety and courteous treatment.

She was not well throughout the heated debates, having developed a fever during her journey to Estremoz. When the compromises were drawn up and signed by Alfonso and Ferdinand, Elizabeth collapsed. She died in the royal tent on the battlefield, as thousands of hardened warriors wept and knelt around her.

Their "Peacemaker," whom they lovingly called Isabella in their own language, was taken to Coimbra, to the Convent of the Poor Clares. Her canonization took place in 1626, and her feast day was set on July 8.

Chapter 8

Francis Xavier

The world has long marveled at the journeys of the original Apostles who were sent by Christ to preach the Gospel, the "Good News," to the peoples of all the countries of the world. The records of their travels are astonishing, and the shrines that honor their labors in many distant lands proclaim their faithfulness to Jesus.

In the sixteenth century, another apostle appeared, and his missionary sojourns stagger the mind, especially if one understands conditions at the time and the modes of travel available. In the 1500s, one did not take a jet plane to distant countries. There were no travel agents, posh hotels, or bed-and-breakfast inns. The ships of that era were fragile and small, hardly luxury liners where guests partied all night or stood at the rail to embrace in the glow of the sunset.

Despite the lack of comforts and the dangers involved, a saint variously called the "Apostle of the Indies," "the Apostle of Japan," and even "the Apostle of the Philippines," managed to undertake some really fantastic journeys that touched the lives of thousands of human beings. He performed most of his travels and contacts within a space of ten years, a mere decade of human existence, and today his spirit lives on in remote and distant cities where his words blend in the tropical heat of the day and rise with the moon over the exotic seas.

The apostle was Saint Francis Xavier, born Francisco de Jassu y Javier, on April 7, 1506, in Xavier Castle in Navarre, Spain. His parents were Basques (meaning they came from the mountainous Basque region of Spain), having the rank and status of the minor nobility of the region. Such status did not mean much in the royal court of Spain or in the lands of the older, more powerful aristocrats, but in Navarre the family was regarded as the true power and the link to the past. These nobles resided in Xavier Castle, a stone edifice that dominated the countryside and is still visible perched on its rocky crest.

Francis was raised in comfort there, even though the castle appears cold and formal in the modern view. He was well educated, probably by a series of tutors, a custom of such nobles in that era. There were no school systems outside of the religious houses, and nobles did not allow their children to mix with others in any sort of public educational institution. Certainly tutors were available for hire, and it was safe for the young heirs to remain at home, where they could be directed by their elders.

In 1525, having learned all that the tutors could teach him, Francis went to Paris, which was a cultural and educational center in Europe at the time, and he enrolled in the College of Sainte-Barbe, one of the schools of the city. Making friends easily and having a considerable charm that attracted others, he enjoyed Paris and the challenges that college life offered him and his classmates. What he intended as his vocation in life is not known, as he probably had obligations to perform in his own family's holdings. Such plans, however, were never realized by Francis or his parents, because he was introduced to an individual who would change his life for all time: Saint Ignatius Loyola.

Ignatius Loyola was in Paris to study, but he also had another vision in mind, one that he believed would aid the Church in a time of great need. He was in the process of founding the Society of Jesus, the order of priests that would eventually be called the Jesuits. Ignatius was quite impressed with Francis Xavier, and he spoke of his vision to him and to several other young men, asking them to join him in this spiritual adventure.

The whole idea must have sounded strange to Francis when he first heard of the new religious order, but in time he became an enthusiastic follower of Ignatius Loyola. Ignatius and Francis were joined by Pierre Favre and four others named Lainez, Salmeron, Rodríguez, and Bobadilla in making the first foundation. They made their first vows at Montmarte (the site of Saint Denis's ordeals) on August 15, 1534.

As a trainee for the new order, Francis completed his education in Paris and then taught at the university. He then went with Ignatius and the others to Venice, where on June 24, 1537, they were ordained into the priesthood of the Church. A year later the first Jesuits were in

Rome, undergoing the *Exercises* (spiritual programs) that would prepare them for strengthening the Jesuit order and spreading the faith.

Learned, holy, and well-disciplined, the Jesuits clearly explained their purpose at the Vatican, impressing Pope Paul III. He saw the need for such an army of spiritual soldiers, and he gave papal approval to the Jesuits, enabling them to begin their mission in the world.

After a brief period of rejoicing, Francis and the others did just that, undertaking the duties of the priesthood and willing to go wherever Almighty God led them. Francis Xavier started out his mission by going to the city of Lisbon in 1540, where King John III of Portugal asked him to accept an assignment in the Far East, in what were called the East Indies. This exotic, newly opened area excited treasure seekers, traders, explorers, adventurers, and missionaries of the Church. Even though India and its neighboring countries had been inhabited for centuries by sophisticated cultures, the Europeans looked upon them as a raw wilderness of delights and mysteries that would offer up rare experiences for those brave enough to reach that distant shore.

King John III of Portugal was too practical and too pious to believe the adventurer's tales, and he had no desire to send out a pack of tradesmen or merchants. Such individuals were there already, he explained, and they needed pastoral care, the sort of guidance and concern that only a priest could provide. What actually mattered to this ruler was the simple fact that Portugal had a foothold in India, in the Goa region. The Portuguese needed missionaries not only for parishes already established but for the millions of Indian people who had never heard of Christ and the Church. Francis Xavier, a representative of a newly founded order, could aid Portugal and the faith by accepting the royal invitation to start his priestly life on the Indian shore.

Accepting John III's request, and receiving permission from Ignatius Loyola, Francis set sail for India, arriving in Goa on May 6, 1542. The trip had been long and difficult, with an ever-changing sky, gusting winds, and countless new tropical horizons coming into view. Francis was eager to reach his destination, eager as well to start a new life of service. He accepted the price of his apostolate. He had committed himself to dwell among strangers in an alien land for years.

Because he was facing the unknown, he did not know if he would ever see his beloved homeland or his family again.

During his first weeks in Goa, Francis introduced himself to the Christians in the area and then set about visiting the sick. He walked through the streets ringing a bell to attract attention, an activity that seems to have caught the fancy of the local inhabitants. India, of course, was quite used to the sight of holy men wandering through the various regions, and they had a natural compassion and interest in such individuals. To the people of the area, Francis Xavier was another holy man.

When he had gathered a group of interested bystanders as a result of walking the streets and ringing a bell, he took them into a nearby parish church or mission and gave them catechetical lessons, meaning he began to teach them about the Catholic faith. This proved successful, and he saw lapsed Catholics returning and new converts coming into the Church.

The Portuguese sailors spending leave from their trading ships in the city turned deaf ears to his pleas for reforming their lives. It would take more than a priest with a bell to bring them around. Also, the local Indian rulers were not entirely thrilled with the sudden upsurge of Catholicism. The Church represented European ways in the minds of these rulers, most of whom were devout Hindus, and they were not going to allow such influences to sway their people, at least not without a fight. Francis listened to their complaints but continued his work.

He was being drawn to yet other lands, where the sun and the sea blended in horizons of fiery red against the backdrop of mountain crests. The Goa complex was doing well, he knew, and its ties with Portugal would keep it safe in the years to come. Beyond, however, where the sea met the sky in a blaze of color at the close of each day, new lands and new peoples waited for him and for Christ.

Then the pearl fishermen in the south sent word to him, and Francis placed the Goa operations in good hands and started on another journey, reaching the beautiful regions of Ceylon (modern-day Sri Lanka) before he was through. These pearl fishermen lived beside the ocean in small villages. They went out each day in boats, diving without air hoses to the oyster beds at the bottom of lagoons and coves, risking their lives with each descent. Able to dive down incredible distances and to go without air for almost superhuman intervals, these men and women gathered up the oysters in baskets each day. Surfacing, they gave the baskets to other workers who opened each oyster, seeking the precious orbs created within the shells.

After three years of missionary work in the area, Francis went to Melaka, in modern Malaysia, to continue recruiting converts. In 1545, he sailed to the Molucca Islands in eastern Indonesia as well. He is also believed to have visited the island of Mindanao in the Philippines, but that part of the journey has not been documented enough to have historical certainty.

Affairs in Goa took a turn for the worse during his absence, and Francis received word that the mission required his attention. He retraced his steps, returning to India where he put an end to quarrels and rivalries so that the mission could prosper once more. By 1548, he knew that he could leave the mission again safely. The Catholic presence in the city was so firmly entrenched that he felt he could seek new lands. He also believed that God had sent him a sign about his next destination.

While restoring order to the mission, Francis had met a Japanese man called Anger (or Han-Sir), which must have been a translation in Indian or Portuguese of his original Japanese name. This Japanese convert to the Church would eventually be given the Christian name of Pablo de Santa Fe, and he would prove invaluable to the mission of Francis Xavier.

Speaking about his native land, the Japanese encouraged Francis to journey there to bring Christ to the people. He spoke of the beautiful islands that made up the nation of Japan, of its exquisite art and traditions, and he explained the samurai, the warriors of the various clans who were constantly at war with one another. The people of Japan were caught in a storm of such wars, waiting for one lord to prove himself victorious and to unite the islands. Now was the time to introduce Christ to the Land of the Rising Sun, as Japan was called. The island nation needed Francis Xavier, and it was time for him to make the long sea journey to its shores.

In 1549, Francis made that treacherous voyage, accompanied by his Japanese friend and by Father Cosme de Torres and Brother Juan Fernandez. They landed in Kagoshima on the island of Kyushu on August 15, 1549. There Francis spent months learning the language and the strange customs. He also introduced himself to local officials and made an effort to visit Kyoto, the capital, without success. He began making so many converts in Kagoshima after beginning his missionary work that he was banished from that city, going to Yamaguchi and then to Honshu Island.

Francis wandered about as a hermit and storyteller for a time, something that attracted the Japanese people, who proved courteous and generous in their hospitality; but he then realized that it was better to claim his Portuguese connections and to ask the Japanese authorities for help and protection.

He understood the Japanese people and spoke of Japan as a fertile missionary territory, saying: "There our holy faith might be spread with great success; there more than any other country . . . were great things to be hoped for. . . ."

Having baptized some two thousand Japanese, Francis Xavier returned to Goa in 1552, because of difficulties there again. He had baptized some ten thousand men and women in Goa during his missionary work in that city and could not abandon them, reporting: "Often my arms are weary from baptizing, and I cannot speak another word from having so repeatedly recited the prayers to the people, one after another."

With the Goa mission settled finally, this time placed in mature and experienced hands, Francis Xavier set out yet another time. He was actually planning to start Catholic missions in China, the mysterious land so long closed to most foreigners. Although such a journey would mean a dangerous sea voyage again, poor food, stale water, and storms, he started his last apostolic mission with a young Chinese companion.

Francis Xavier left Goa in April of 1552 and came within sight of the Chinese mainland before collapsing, his labors having taken their toll. Francis had spent an entire decade working for souls in foreign lands, and the stress of new faces and new languages, the opposition from government officials, and the perils of traveling in that era had brought about his physical decline. On December 3, 1552, he died on the island of Shangchuen (Sancian).

His body was returned to Goa immediately and placed in a chapel of a convent there as the entire population mourned the passing of this great apostle. The flesh on his dead body remained miraculously preserved, attesting to his favor with God and impressing countless numbers of men and women who visited his shrine.

Saint Francis Xavier was the greatest of all Christian missionaries since Saint Paul. He traveled thousands of miles, confronting strange lands, customs, and languages, and using an interpreter when he could not make himself understood by his mission flocks. Because he had little money, no organization, and often faced opposition, he won over the native populations of many lands by living with them and sharing their sorrows and joys.

With Saint Ignatius Loyola, Francis Xavier was canonized by Pope Gregory XV. He was proclaimed patron of all foreign missions by Pope Saint Pius X, and his feast day is observed on December 3.

Gabriel the Archangel

Chapter 9

Gabriel the Archangel

In this particular age, when everyone is talking about angels, heaven, and the afterlife, Saint Gabriel the Archangel stands as a contradiction to the popular theories being discussed. Several publications about angels describe the heavenly host as cute, charming, loving, helpful, and kindly creatures whose sole purpose in the universe is to make humans feel better about themselves and one another. Behold Gabriel, who bears many celestial titles and has been included in many religious traditions over the centuries as a powerful being who performs the will of God!

His name is translated as "the Strength of the Lord" or as "the Lord is my Strength," which denotes, or makes evident, his special standing and his heavenly roles. Gabriel, in fact, carries many traditional aspects, considered both an angel of punishment and an angel of mercy in heaven's dealings with humankind.

In truth, angels are very complex forms of creation that cannot be put into categories easily or quickly. Thinking of angels as only the companions or helpmates of humans is not only illogical but insulting to the wondrous nature of angels. The roles of these members of the heavenly choirs were decreed by Almighty God and go far beyond anything that humans can understand or possibly imagine in their wildest dreams. Also, such angels may have a certain allure or attractiveness, especially in this period of history when virtues and goodness are under attack; but they are the servants of God, not superstars on their own.

The word angel comes from *angiras*, a Sanskrit term. Sanskrit is the language used centuries ago in India. The Persians had their own varieties of angels, and they called them *angaros*. The Greeks believed such creatures were messengers and named them *angelos* (meaning messenger), from which the modern name is derived.

Angels do serve as messengers. In fact, in many of the recorded appearances of angels, such as those recorded in the Old and New Testaments, they were announcing something or other to humans, stating something of divine purpose, not just standing around passing the time of day.

Now all of the paintings and stone statues of angels portray these pure spirits in totally human form, making them easy to recognize and artistically beautiful. They are shown with physical bodies, and they wear the clothes that were considered highly fashionable in certain eras. The wings and halos provided for them in such portraits reminded viewers that these creatures are not earth-bound but members of the "realms of glory" far beyond mortal men and women and their fads.

The Church teaches that angels are beings of pure spirit, created by God and destined by him for his own purposes. Because humans like to define things, to know what makes things work, many writers and saintly thinkers over the years have tried to figure out how the angels might be organized so as to serve the Almighty in the best way possible. These writers, using Scripture and ancient customs, created what are called angelic orders, listings of angelic ranks according to their tasks and attributes.

These orders are also beautifully called choirs, expressing one of their very important duties: They surround the throne of the Lord and sing his praises to all of the heavens. This activity is not boring to the angels at all; in fact, it is one of their favorite and cherished roles because they understand that they were created by the Almighty, and unlike humans, they are filled with everlasting gratitude. Some of the great mystics of the Church have tried to tell their fellow human beings that the role of everyone in heaven will be to imitate the angels in giving praise. The mystics ask why modern mortals do not begin that vocation while still on earth. Such praise would link men and women on the earth with the heavenly choirs.

In the list of the "angelic choirs," as they are called, there are nine separate groupings: from the highest to the lowest, they are the Seraphim, Cherubim, Thrones, Dominions, Virtues, Powers, Principalities, Archangels, and Angels. Sometimes, the list can make things a little confusing. For example, all of the members of God's angelic host are generally called angels by human beings, but there is also an order called Angels. Also, the greatest leaders of the whole heavenly host are called archangels, even though the second lowest of the angelic choirs are also Archangels. Experts in angels, however, see these as minor points and consider the titles of the angels as mere descriptions of the beauty and love reflected by all of the angels who belong to each group.

The Angels, members of the ninth heavenly choir, are the lowest-ranked beings in such celestial circles. They serve as messengers in the world, as guardians of people and places, and as an inspiration for each new generation upon the earth. Above them are the Archangels, the members of the eighth choir. Archangels serve in much the same way as Angels, but when they announce something, it is a "divine decree" — in other words, from God himself.

Higher than the Angels and Archangels are the Principalities. These are the beings of the seventh choir of heaven, sometimes called the Princedoms. Such powerful creatures are entrusted by God with the protection of the faith and with the care of righteous leaders in human affairs. The Principalities inspire such leaders to make right and moral decisions.

The sixth choir of heaven is composed of the Powers, or Potentates. Their purpose in God's plan is to maintain order on the road to heaven and to ensure that demons and other evil creatures cannot overcome the world, no matter how much such devils plot the downfall of good.

The Virtues form the fifth choir, and they are really splendid beings who concern themselves with all of the miracles taking place upon earth. The Virtues are entrusted by God to bring his grace to men and women everywhere, and in times of crisis, they provide the faithful with enough courage and fortitude to overcome evil in their lives.

The Dominions (or Dominations) make up the fourth choir and are part of the real hierarchy, or upper levels, of heaven. Carrying scepters and orbs (an "orb" is a fancy name for a round ball), the Dominions express God's glory. This choir gives constant praise to God and regulates the activities of the various levels of heaven.

Above the Dominions are heavenly beings called Thrones. They form the third choir of spirits and are very powerful. The Thrones are sometimes called the "Many-Eyed Ones," a title referring to their alertness and their ability to see everything that is going on in God's universe. Thrones make God's justice evident in the world. In other words, they promote the law and the obligations that all created beings have in the presence of the Deity, or God.

In the second choir, the Cherubim represent God's glory and goodness in splendor. Cherubim are powerful beings who perform special tasks. They were sent to guard the Tree of Life in the Garden of Eden, and they were equipped with fiery swords in order to perform their divine assignments. Two Cherubim were also carved on the Ark of the Covenant to protect the broken remains of the Ten Commandments.

Highest in rank and in honor is the first choir of heaven, the Seraphim. These truly magnificent beings circle the throne of Almighty God, endlessly chanting what is called the Trisagion: *Sanctus Sanctus, Sanctus, Dominus Deus Sabaoth* ("Holy, Holy, Holy, Lord God of the Hosts"). The Seraphim are the most wondrous and awesome of all angels, occupying the cherished place closest to the Lord's throne. They are described as having four faces and six wings. It is safe to assume that if you had ever met a Seraphim, you would never recover from the shock.

Now above the Angels are the mighty Princes of heaven, also called Archangels, who serve as the chiefs of the choirs and the special ministers of God. They include many Angels who are renowned around the world, such as Raphael and Michael; others are not very well known and are said to be figures largely of legend, such as Uriel, Metatron, and Camael. Of the Archangels, the three revered by the Church are Michael, Raphael, and Gabriel.

The Archangel Gabriel is more than a member of the eighth choir of heaven. He is also considered a member of the first order, the Seraphim, and is called a Prince of Heaven, the Angel of Justice, the Angel of Mercy, and an Angel of Destruction. In other words, Gabriel has more on his angelic mind than helping little old ladies across busy street corners.

He is one of three heavenly beings mentioned in the Bible, with Michael and Raphael. But Gabriel is recorded as making appearances in both the Old and New Testaments, ever involved by divine will in the affairs of human redemption and salvation.

In the Old Testament, Gabriel explains a dream to the prophet Daniel, and he is also described in a biblical account in the Book of Daniel. In the New Testament, the Archangel has some extremely important tasks. He is believed to be the heavenly messenger who announced the birth of Saint John the Baptist and then served as the messenger another time, at the Annunciation. This means he was the blessed spirit who appeared to the Virgin Mary to receive her consent in bringing Jesus into the world.

Now here lies the contradiction of Gabriel, demonstrating the wide range of his concerns and tasks on earth. He is called the Angel of Justice and Judgment, reflecting God's will and the last ends of all mortal beings. He is described as being surrounded by thunder and symbols of majesty. When the world comes to an end, Gabriel will be the one to sound the dreaded trumpet that will signal the final destruction and the appearance of Christ as the Judge of good and evil upon the earth.

Gabriel is also believed to have been one of the angels who destroyed the evil cities of Sodom and Gomorrah, which explains his title as an Angel of Destruction. In that role he also wiped out, single-handedly, the 185,000-man army of the Assyrian Empire, which threatened God's Chosen People.

He was probably the heavenly being who wrestled with Jacob in the Old Testament account, and may have been the angel who took part in the burial of Moses. Saint Joan of Arc said that Gabriel was among the spirits who visited her and urged her to undertake the military campaigns against the English that helped free France during the long struggle called the Hundred Years' War.

He has yet other roles in the affairs of ordinary men and women. A pious story has it that, as the Angel of Birth, he watches over the unborn babies, training their developing spirits. Gabriel touches these babies on the lips with his fingertip just before they are born, which is, the story goes on, why humans have slight clefts between their lips and noses.

Above all, Gabriel is the Angel of Mercy, who announced the Incarnation, the coming of Christ into the world, the true consolation of human beings everywhere, in every age. He was thus close to the Holy Family, possibly appearing to Saint Joseph, the husband of the Blessed Virgin. He was also believed to be a member of the choir of heavenly host that announced the birth of Jesus to the shepherds in Bethlehem.

Gabriel's symbol is the lily, the flower of purity and the insignia of the resurrection of Christ. His feast day is celebrated on September 29 and is shared by the Archangels Michael and Raphael.

Chapter 10

Hedwig

The daily news reports about wars and suffering in modern
European regions are teaching people everywhere that some areas on
that restless continent have always been troubled. Religious and
political conflicts have engulfed them for centuries as the problems of
the region that used to be called Yugoslavia demonstrate. The feuds
and rivalries evident there date back to medieval times, when many
regions in Europe were not only torn apart by ambitions and creeds
but threatened by invasion from the East. Thus there were not many
peaceful times in Europe, and some of them were more dangerous
than others, as the life of Hedwig clearly demonstrates.

Saint Hedwig, also known as Jadwiga, was born in the region
known as the Balkans, the same territory that has grabbed the
attention of the world with its suffering and strife in modern times. If
that wasn't bad enough, she was destined to marry into yet another
area of political turmoil, facing the perils and sufferings brought about
by wars.

She entered the world sometime around 1174, and she grew up
in a time of strife and unrest when her land was endangered and
learned early that God demands that saints rise and flourish especially
in times of pain and anguish, because that is when their examples are
most needed.

Hedwig was the daughter of a nobleman named Berthold IV, the
count of Andechs and duke of Croatia and Dalmatia. She was one of
eight children born into the ducal family, sharing the pleasures and
privileges of her aristocratic childhood with brothers and sisters. Upon
reaching school age, as was the custom of the time, she was placed in
a cloister in Kitzingen, to be trained by the nuns for her coming
obligations.

Her stay in the cloister was rather brief because she was given in marriage at the age of twelve to Henry I, the duke of Silesia. Because most people did not expect to live long in that day and age, they set about their activities early, hoping to get a head start, so to speak.

Henry belonged to a strong and reliable family that would leave its mark on history in time. Silesia, his holdings, was a Polish province on the Oder River, and he ruled it with an enlightened point of view and a sense of decency and honor. In the ninth century, Silesia had been dominated by Slavic tribes that introduced their culture into the region. The tribes of the people called the Czechs moved in one hundred years later, only to face a Polish army that claimed the land and proved itself victorious enough in battle to take power.

As the ranking lord of that much-disputed (or fought-over) territory, Henry was energetic and genuinely interested in improving everyone's lot in life. He believed that the solution to his problems in renewing ideas and industry could be found in all things German. The Germanic approach to life appealed to him because he had seen how things worked under German rule. As a result, he decided to introduce Germanic ways to his land. Looking about for a woman from the noble families who might be suitable and in agreement with his plans, Henry chose Hedwig.

During the Middle Ages, it was common for a noble or even a royal family to choose wives and husbands for their children, not in the hopes of making their sons and daughters happy, but to strengthen bonds, political ties, and forge alliances. Marriages were not entered into because a young couple met and fell in love, but out of political or military need. A noble might send his daughter to wed another noble because her father hoped to garner the support and friendship of someone much stronger, with more lands and more troops. It was always a good idea to have friends and allies because you never knew when some other lord might hungrily eye your fields and towns and decide to attack. The more friends — especially powerful ones — that a noble might have, the safer he would be.

Children were thus a helpful way of cementing ties to others who could provide advantages. After all, the son-in-law of a local lord might hesitate to burn down the castle of his wife's parents. Sisters and brothers also formed bonds as young children, and these could be counted upon to defend some of the local lands. These brothers and sisters may rival one another, even fight like a pack of wild dogs, but they united quickly against a common enemy. If they were married to noble houses in the neighborhood, they could present a rather alarming front against anyone deciding to invade.

Well trained in the cloister and made to understand the rules of life and marriage at the time, Hedwig accepted her marriage to Henry and proved to be a prudent and pious duchess, despite her young age. Such women had many responsibilities and duties, forcing them to grow up very quickly.

She knew how to manage the huge army of servants in the ducal palaces and maintained order in the household. Most women of her station (meaning her place as duchess) wore rings of keys at their waists, including the keys to storage areas, pantries, kitchens, bakeries, stockyards, and gardens. Those with energy and real interest in the life of the people made the rounds of the various towns and villages under their domain, or rule, seeing to better conditions there and making provisions for the desperately poor and ill. They usually gave a few coins or necessities to the poor and made short talks that would assure everyone around that the lord and lady of the manor did care, even if they couldn't get around to doing anything about the basic problems facing the peasants. The peasants, or serfs, were used to such blather, but in Hedwig's case they believed her because she had the look of a saint.

Hedwig went far beyond the usual ceremonies or vague promises of aid and comfort. She not only traveled to all of the corners of her husband's lands but also stopped at every hut and half-ruined hovel to ask what she could do to assist the people living there. She gave them money, brought clothing and food, and prayed for and with the starving and downtrodden. In her time, there were many who were ill, suffering, and seemingly forgotten by the world; and she told them that they were not alone, and that Christ loved each and every one of them. To help the Church, she founded convents and monasteries, with Henry's approval, inviting into the duchy the many religious orders, such as the Cistercians. Her devotion to the Cistercians was so great that one of her children, Gertrude, entered the order's convent for women and eventually became an abbess of one of the abbeys founded by Henry and Hedwig.

Aside from Hedwig's labors for the lowest in the duchy, she shared a full life with her husband in the ducal residence at Breslau, now in modern Poland. The couple had seven children, but one son and two daughters died as infants, since the mortality rate (the number of people who died) was much higher for babies in that era. One son, named Conrad, showed promise, but he died at a young age when he was thrown from a horse after a quarrel with another son, Henry II, who became the heir to his father. Gertrude became a nun, and another son, Boleslaw, grew up in the palace. After the birth of Boleslaw, Hedwig and Henry both took vows of perpetual chastity. Their vows were part of their deep devotion to the faith, so much so that they gave up all interest in matters of the flesh as a sacrifice to God. Henry grew a beard, earning the name "the Bearded," and he lived as a layman in the order of Cistercians. Hedwig, meanwhile, devoted most of her time to the Cistercian convent where her daughter lived.

Their spiritual development did not bring an end to their worldly involvements, however; and, from time to time, political troubles intruded on their prayerful lives. In 1227, for example, Henry was ambushed and wounded by a rival lord, and Hedwig rushed to his side to nurse him back to health. Then, in a feud over the city of Cracow, Henry was taken prisoner while attending a church service, an act considered a blasphemy by most of the people at the time. His captor, Conrad of Marovia, a man who obviously did not give much thought to blasphemy or the Church as a sanctuary for rich and poor alike, held Henry as his prisoner. Conrad probably would have killed Henry, because he was that sort of individual, had Hedwig not arrived on the scene to plead for his release. At the sight of her, Conrad relented and allowed Henry his freedom. At her insistence, the two also sat down, face to face, to make a compromise between them to end their rivalries. They both swore to keep the peace, a fact that made a lot of people feel good about things.

Silesia was thus secure until 1238, when Duke Henry died. Hedwig buried him with the solemn rites of the Church and then retired permanently to the Cistercian convent. She was happy to be entering the last phase of her life there, and she cherished the routines of the convent and the prayers.

Hedwig stayed in the convent of the Cistercians until 1241, when she departed to bring help and encouragement to her people in the face of yet another disaster. Out of the East one of the most feared invaders of all time, the Mongols, were cutting deep paths of blood and destruction in Europe. These wild and terrible horsemen had swept out of their lands in modern Mongolia to drive westward under the leadership of their chiefs, called khans, descendants of the famous conqueror Genghis Khan. The Mongols burned and looted cities all over Russia and were threatening Poland and Austria, two bastions, like Russia, of the Christian faith. The people in those regions were naturally hysterical at the thought of what was happening, and women like Hedwig had to calm them and bring sense and faith into play.

With the prayers of Hedwig going with her son Henry II, now duke, Henry set out with his troops to do battle with the onrushing Mongols. He rode into battle with a host of other Christian knights. They met the Mongols at a place called Liegnitz. There they would make their stand in defense of Christendom, as Europe was called. The Mongols, though, proved far too strong. In one afternoon, the entire army of knights and archers was massacred. Nearly every Christian soldier was killed in the fray, or fight, including Hedwig's beloved son Henry.

All of Poland had prayed night and day that they might be spared the coming disaster. Stories had already spread about the deep suffering endured by the Russian people. When word of the Battle of Liegnitz reached their ears, the Polish people wept in grief and fear, for it seemed that nothing would save them from the fury of the Mongols. For Hedwig, this was a double blow, for not only had she lost her son, she knew that many young men had died in battle, all with families, friends, and loved ones who would never see them again.

The prayers of the anguished Poles — and many others throughout Europe — did not go unanswered. Hedwig and all of the prayerful rejoiced at the news that the Mongols had suddenly stopped and were turning around to go home. Despite having crushed an entire Christian army, they could not take advantage of their superior military powers, could not invade Poland or Austria because their highest ruler, called the Great Khan, had died quite unexpectedly back on the plains of Mongolia. As was the custom among the Mongols, all of the khans had to return home to choose a successor. Never going anywhere without their huge armies, the khans ended their campaigns and set out for the East. Thus with the church bells tolling and the cities and towns of the region filled with deliriously happy men and women singing praises and songs of thanksgiving to God, Hedwig joined in the celebrations, even while she never forgot her son Henry or his many fallen comrades.

She lived only two years after the death of Henry II on the

battlefield. Probably weakened by the loss of her son, she never fully recovered her health. She died on October 15, 1243, and the people of Silesia mourned her passing. She was canonized in 1267 by Pope Clement IV and declared the patroness of her adopted land. Her feast is October 16.

Chapter 11

Jude

The Twelve Apostles, the truly blessed individuals chosen by Christ to accompany him on his mission in the world, remain forever a vital part of the Christian heritage and tradition. They were not scholars or famous preachers when Christ first picked them to join him. They were not politically powerful men or renowned soldiers or generals. Our Lord, the Second Person of the Blessed Trinity, called average human beings from their normal commonplace routines to walk with him, to partake in his earthly existence, and to spread the Christian faith.

Some were fishermen, like Saint Peter, the first pope and the Rock on whom Christ would build his Church; another was a tax collector, Matthew, whom the Lord called away from his money tables. They were all simple men, but each would be set on fire within his soul as a result of living, walking, and laboring with Christ. They would also set out on their own missions in time and joyfully take to the road that led, ultimately, to a blessed martyrdom.

Such men would live with Christ, would hear him preach the Good News of salvation. They would witness Christ's miracles and would receive the Holy Spirit at Pentecost. The Apostles were not instant saints or martyrs. As the Gospels relate, they were afraid in times of danger and filled with doubts and unsure of themselves in their world of the spirit. Still, they remained loyal in good times and in bad, and they allowed themselves to be fashioned into the sort of humans who could endure persecution and the sword — thus becoming inspirations for countless generations on earth.

Saint Jude, called Thaddeus by some, probably to make certain that no one would confuse him for the traitor Judas Iscariot, was just such an Apostle. Still, he remains one of the most obscure, or hidden, of the companions of Christ, even to this very day. Very little is known about him actually. No one wrote an explanation of how Jude met Jesus, and there is no word of Jude's occupation before becoming an Apostle. Even less has been proven about his martyrdom or death.

Saint Jude Thaddeus was an individual who was on the scene but not shining or in the spotlight, the sort of person that nowadays might be called "just another face in the crowd." However, he is also one of the most popular saints in the modern world. He is known as the patron of "hopeless cases," which could well describe most of the men and women walking around today, a fact that makes him popular.

Jude is listed in the Gospel of Saint Luke and in the Acts of the Apostles as Judas of James. In the Gospels written by Saint Mark and Saint Matthew he is called Thaddeus. In Saint John's Gospel he is known as "Judas (not Iscariot)" to make clear to the reader, as pointed out above, that he was not related in any way to the traitor. In time the world came to know him simply as Jude, to protect him even more from the terrible reputation of Judas Iscariot, and to give him his proper place as a faithful follower of Christ.

Jude was most likely the brother of the Apostle called James the Lesser. It is quite possible that he just tagged along when James met the Lord and was accepted. No one made mention of the first meeting between him and Jesus, even though that encounter certainly changed Jude's life for all time.

This lack of information or historical references, of course, makes Jude a rather shadowy figure, one who had the misfortune of sharing his name with a man who would be cursed forever. Without question, however, the first meeting was one in which Christ looked upon Jude and perceived in him one of those he would call to join him in his work. Christ knew that Jude, like his fellow disciples, possessed the goodness of heart and soul to be deserving of the companionship of the Son of Man, one of the greatest honors ever bestowed upon members of the human race. Jude listened and responded to both the call of Christ and to the challenge he was offering. Jude, like the other Apostles, had to believe enough to give up everything he had known, all he had cared for and loved, and to embark upon a glorious spiritual adventure even in the face of scorn or persecution.

The one vivid account of Jude that is included in the Gospels portrays him as asking a rather logical question of the Savior at the Last Supper. At this final meal, Jesus would warn the disciples of what was coming and would institute the Holy Eucharist for Christians everywhere in the centuries ahead.

Gathered at the table with the others, and probably getting up enough nerve to ask the same thing that the rest wondered about, Jude asked Christ why he had revealed himself in his fullness to the disciples but not to the world. Such a question shows that Jude thought about Christ's mission and about the men and women around him. He lived in a difficult age, when simple families were at the mercy of the ruler of the world, Rome, as well as corrupt local petty kings, political leaders, and tax collectors who mercilessly gathered funds for their Roman masters. Would Jesus speak to them all, openly in time? Christ's answer to Jude was a simple one: He and the Father would visit all who loved and obeyed them.

It is not clear what Jude did during the terrible hours of the Passion, in which Christ was arrested, tried, and finally crucified by the Romans. He was probably hiding and shaking in his boots — or should we say, "trembling in his sandals"? — like the rest of the other Apostles. It is known that he was present in the days after Christ's death on the cross, seeing proof with the other Apostles of the Resurrection and the Ascension. He was there as well when the followers of Christ received the Holy Spirit at Pentecost.

The Church, given birth by the Holy Spirit, needed missionaries to spread the word. Once again, Jude, with his brother in the Lord, accepted and took up the challenge of Christ to go into the world and bring about the salvation of all peoples.

Jude traveled with Saint James, another Apostle, and according to historical records reached Persia (now modern Iran), which was a long way from Jerusalem. The Persians were no more open to Christianity in that age than they are now. Persia was not a Muslim country at the time, and its people believed instead in ancient gods of their own. They were not thrilled to see another faith arriving in their lands, judging it to be a foreign religion and too different from their older religious customs, which were based on the creed known as Zoroastrianism (or Mazdaism).

Jude is also known for writing an epistle, a fancy word for letter. But that letter remains at the center of yet another controversy concerning Jude's authorship. In it the Apostle warned about false prophets and urges loyalty to the faith. Jude writes: "But you, beloved, build yourselves up on your most holy faith; pray in the Holy Spirit;

keep yourselves in the love of God; wait for the mercy of our Lord Jesus Christ unto eternal life. And convince some, who doubt; save some, by snatching them out of the fire; on some have mercy with fear. . ." (20-23).

The letter is signed "Jude, a servant of Jesus Christ and brother of James." Now that certainly identifies Jude, but scholars argue about the date on which it was written, some claiming that, because of the date, the letter could not possibly have been written by the Apostle Jude.

It is known that Jude was martyred in Persia, with Saint Simon. Normally, Jude is portrayed holding a club, as the Persians beat him to death when he tried to inform them about Christ. In a similar way, Saint Simon is seen holding a saw, because his Persian executioners cut him to pieces with saws as they were murdering Jude. Their deaths are recorded in a work called the *Passion of Simon and Jude*, although experts say that this writing is unreliable as a truthful source on the martyrdoms. In the eighth century, the relics (or remains) of the saints were recovered from their place of burial and taken to St. Peter's in Rome. Interestingly, two other cities, Reims and Toulouse, in France, both claimed to have some of the remains of the saints as well.

Jude slowly became honored over the centuries as the patron saint of hopeless cases. It apparently started with the account given in John's Gospel concerning "Judas (not Iscariot)." Many of the faithful over the years did not know of this statement, so they remained confused about his true identity and therefore uncertain about asking Jude for help. They would run the lists of the saints for their intercession in various crises, asking the entire host of the canonized for help. If they received no relief from their problems, many finally decided to give Jude a try as their last hope.

He responded to the hopeless with speed and with concern, and more and more Christians learned to count on him as a true friend, especially in urgent or critical cases. Word spread and shrines developed to honor his intercessions on behalf of the living. Today one of the finest children's hospitals in the world bears his name. Saint Jude shares a feast day with Saint Simon on October 28.

Kateri Jekakwitha

Chapter 12

Kateri Tekakwitha

More than a century before the United States of America became a nation, the Lily of the Mohawks, Kateri Tekakwitha, was chosen by God to be a vessel of his grace in the wilderness of the New World. She was a Mohawk Indian, even though the term "Indian" is not accurate to describe the Native American people. The term came into being because Christopher Columbus did not have a clue as to where he was heading with his tiny fleet of ships.

He sailed out of Spain intending to reach the "Indies" — the name given to the fabled East — once visited by Marco Polo. When Columbus sighted land after a long voyage, he naturally thought that he had reached the Indies. No one had told him that a giant continent, the one to be named America, rose out of the ocean halfway between Europe and the Orient. Columbus was convinced that he had reached his destination, so he called the local inhabitants "Indians."

Kateri's people were part of the Five Nations Confederacy, a union that started with the vision of an Iroquois named Dekanawidah, or Tekanawita. He prayed over the suffering of his people when they made war upon one another, and had a vision of a Tree of Great Peace, around which the chiefs (or sachems) of the Mohawks, Oneidas, Cayugas, Onondagas, and the Senecas met to decide matters of the region. In time the Tuscaroras would also join this union. The tribes became the Ho-den-na-sau-nee, the People of the Longhouses. The "longhouse" was a division of land running from north to south; it received its name from the long dwellings, or houses, in which combined Indian families lived. When put together, the Five Nations controlled the land stretching from the Hudson River in New York to the shores of Lake Erie. To the misfortune of white settlers trying to enter Iroquoia, as the region was called, the Mohawks lived in the easternmost "longhouse," and they were not enthusiastic about seeing white men strolling across their lands.

Benjamin Franklin used the Five Nations Confederacy as a model when he urged the colonies to unite for defense and trade. There were about twenty-five thousand in the Five Nations Confederacy in the mid-1600s, when French trappers started into the area. With that population and a united response to threatening forces, the Five Nations could put an army of three thousand to four thousand into battle, all trained warriors eager to defend their homelands. Once in the field, these warriors moved with military precision, becoming a terrifying enemy. In the time of the colonies, just a rumor about the approach of these warriors was enough to send colonists screaming and running for cover.

In the Mohawk longhouse, a powerful chief happened to marry a captive Algonquin maiden and took her to his home in Ossernenon. She bore him a daughter in 1656, and the child was named Tekakwitha, which was translated as "she who puts things in order." The Algonquin woman had been raised a Christian, but she probably did not visit the Jesuit missions in the area, since the Mohawks despised the Church because it belonged to the white men.

A son was born three years after Kateri Tekakwitha, and both children were secretly taught hymns and prayers by their mother. The very village where they lived had been the site of the martyrdom of Jesuits: Saint Isaac Jogues, Saint John Lalande, Saint René Goupil, and others of the faith. Kateri was born just a few yards from the sacred ground watered by the blood of the martyrs, and at her mother's knee she was learning about Jesus.

Disaster struck, however, in 1660, when the Mohawks contracted the dread white man's disease called smallpox. Kateri was stricken, and even as she was nursed by kindly Mohawk women, her mother, father, baby brother, and a good many friends perished from the terrible illness.

The matrons, or older women, of the village elected Kateri's uncle as the new war chief. The older women of the tribe had political power, especially in the choice of chiefs. Such women knew these men from their childhood and were considered wise in determining the virtues or vices of each candidate.

Kateri moved in with her uncle, whose wife and sister made her welcome. She also went with them when the tribe moved to a new site, Gandawague. As was the custom, the bodies of Kateri's mother, father, and brother were taken along for reburial in the new village. There she grew up much loved and given care. Her eyes never regained their full sight. She appears to have seen things at close range, but distant things remained dim, and light gave her pain.

By this time the Indians making up the Five Nations Confederacy controlled the wilderness in New York and Ohio, and they controlled the trade routes in Delaware, Maryland, New Jersey, Pennsylvania, northern Virginia, Kentucky, and parts of Illinois, Indiana, and Michigan. Montreal, in Canada, however, remained their spiritual homeland, and they ventured into Canada whenever they felt like it.

Kateri was much beloved by her own Mohawks, especially by the older women who admired her gentle kindness and her willingness to work without complaining. She was also noted for her skill in decorating shirts, mantles, and other pieces of clothing. She seemed to see the patterns in her heart, if not in her eyes.

In June 1677, Kateri's life was about to change again. The arrival of the Blackrobes, as the Jesuit priests were called, started a long series of conversions among the people. The lovely feast-day celebrations, including the manger scenes of Christmas, attracted the Mohawks. Kateri attended some of these festivals, but she made no move toward entering the Church. She had refused to marry any of the young Mohawk warriors, however, a fact that made her people consider her odd, perhaps even unhealthy in the mind. Marriage was an honorable state in the Five Nations.

When the "Dawn of Day" — the name given to Father Jacques de Lamberville (the Jesuit who knew the Mohawks so well) — came to the village mission, life changed for the Indian maiden. He talked to Kateri one day and was startled to hear her ask for baptism. She was actually a high-ranked Mohawk, and her conversion would have a great effect on the others in the village. Also, Kateri seemed to understand prayer, penance, and the presence of God without formal catechism. Father de Lamberville told her she could begin studying the faith but was slow to speak about baptism. Her family agreed to the catechism lessons, and Kateri went to the priest's instruction courses, astounding the Jesuits with her knowledge of the spiritual life.

The day of her baptism, Easter Sunday, 1676, was very special in the village. The Mohawks decorated the chapel specially for the ceremony and many attended out of respect for Kateri. She began her new life in Christ as a true contemplative, which means simply that she experienced "the joyful gaze of her soul upon God." She appeared small and delicate, but in her spirit she was an eagle flying directly to God.

Her long hours of prayer and her continued refusal to marry brought about a response from her uncle and the other Mohawks. Rumors were started by those who did not understand, and one young Mohawk warrior told her to act normal or die. The situation became worse each day, and Father de Lamberville asked God to send him a solution, some way to give Kateri protection.

The answer came in the person of a powerful Oneida chief named Garonhiague but called "Hot Ashes" or "Hot Cinders" by the white man because of his ferocious temper and deadly skills in hunting and battle. Hot Ashes was a Christian, and he was asked by Father de Lamberville to help Kateri get away from her village and into a Christian Indian settlement. Hot Ashes agreed to have his companions take Kateri to the Sault Mission. One of these young men was an Algonquin, a relative of Kateri's dead mother.

The Christian Mohawks sped off with Kateri, but it was not long before the village sounded the alarm that she was missing. Her uncle, who was at a nearby white man's fort, was summoned, and he came racing back, bent on murdering anyone responsible for Kateri's disappearance. He cared about her, and she was a high-ranking Mohawk maiden, the daughter of a dead chief. The uncle's efforts proved in vain. After several narrow escapes from his wrath, Kateri reached the Sault Mission in the fall of 1677. The mission was located on the beautiful Lake St. Paul, where the Portage River emptied into the mighty St. Lawrence. Officially the site was called the Mission of St. Francis Xavier of Sault St. Louis. The word *sault* was French for rapids, or white-water stretches, in the rivers.

There was a chapel on the grounds and priests' residences as well as work areas, all surrounded by a wooden stockade, a high fence. Kateri and the other Native Americans lived in longhouses beside the compound. It is believed that from one hundred twenty to one hundred fifty Native Americans lived at the mission in Kateri's time. The priests in charge were Father Jacques Fremin, Father Pierre Cholenec, and Father Claude Chauchetière. Kateri brought them a letter from Father de Lamberville that informed the priests: "I send you a treasure, guard it well."

Kateri was quite taken by the peace and joy of the community and by the beautiful chapel that was open to all of the Native Americans. Mass started at 4:00 A.M., when the stars were fading and the nearby lake and forests were mantled by mists. Kateri attended two Masses each morning, with the congregation singing hymns in their own language. The Rosary was also recited. In the afternoon they met for Vespers and Benediction of the Blessed Sacrament. Kateri attended all of these services and also prayed in a grove in the woods. At her side was Anastasia, an older woman who had known Kateri's mother.

Kateri received Holy Communion on Christmas Day in 1677, and again her companions decorated the chapel out of affection and love. As she approached the altar, however, many in the chapel were startled. Kateri's plain face took on a glowing light and a new beauty. She was already ill, but receiving Christ in Communion filled her with such joy that her whole being reflected what she was experiencing.

Another woman, Marie Thérèse Tegaiaguenta, came into Kateri's world as her spirit soared and her physical strength faded. Both women prayed together and even asked if they could become nuns. The priests laughed, of course, because it was unthinkable that a Native American might be called to the religious life, at least from a European's point of view. Kateri solved the problem by making a private vow that she would never seek comfort in the arms of a human being and would never depart from Christ. In her soul, Kateri was already far more advanced in prayer, understanding the presence of God and united to him in the way of the truly great mystics of the world.

Her prayers and acts of penance took their toll eventually, and Kateri took to her pallet, a thin stuffed mattress. No longer able to go to the chapel, she was given holy cards by the priests and spent hours looking at them with joy. The other Native Americans, sensing that her spirit was about to break loose from the bonds of the earth, gathered around her. To their astonishment, Kateri told them the secrets of their lives, predicted the future, and warned those whose faith was lukewarm.

The time came, of course, when the priests announced that they would bring her the Church's last rites. Kateri admitted to Marie

Thérèse that she was ashamed to greet Christ in her usual rags, so Marie Thérèse and the other Mohawk women brought her new garments and dressed her lovingly for her final journey. Kateri Tekakwitha died on April 17, 1680, at the age of twenty-four.

The word swept through the settlement and then into the nearby villages. It was a simple message, one understood instantly by Indians and whites alike: "The saint is dead." More and more came to kneel beside her body and they watched as Kateri was transformed. Her skin lost its scars and shadows, glistening as if carved out of pure ivory beside her lustrous dark hair.

Two French trappers who had known Kateri for years happened by at that moment, looking into the longhouse and asking who the beautiful maiden was sleeping there. When they heard that it was Kateri, now passed from the earth, they fell to their knees and wept. These trappers made a wooden coffin for her remains, and she was buried on the bank of the river.

Six days after her death Kateri appeared to a priest of the Sault Mission to warn him of coming events. Anastasia, her friend, saw her radiant and beautiful, and people discovered that the personal effects she had left behind had miraculous healing properties. Her personal items brought renewed strength, relief from pain, even lasting cures.

The Lily of the Mohawks was a mystic who needed no schooling in the art of love and prayer. She was declared Venerable, or worthy of special honor, in 1943, and thirty-seven years later, in 1980, she was declared Blessed. The prayer being recited by people all over the world for her canonization recognizes that Kateri Tekakwitha blossomed in the American wilderness in the company of God and his angels.

Louis IX

Chapter 13

Louis IX

Life in the Middle Ages from around 500 to 1492 was a really strange mixture of good and evil, of faith and crude ambitions, of charitable works and unlimited personal greed. In other words, the people of that historical period wanted the finer things of the spirit and the Christian virtues but too often found themselves swamped by tyrants, warring armies, and kings who were not quite up to the task of governing their nations. The social system of the time, called feudalism, was arranged so that the peasants and serfs — those working the land — sometimes suffered at the hands of the nobles. Good people sometimes worried about that, but life was difficult, and there were so many feuds and wars that people got distracted and let things slide. Kings claimed divine rights, unlimited powers, and the loyalty of everyone in their lands, but they seldom worked hard for this faith and seldom managed to make anyone feel better about having them on the throne.

Saint Louis IX (also known as Saint Louis of France) was therefore rather unique. He was one of the very few monarchs of the era who worried about all levels of society in his land. He introduced what many called a Golden Age in France and became the model for future generations of rulers everywhere.

If one looks at his actual accomplishments, especially during the crusades, Louis was not the most celebrated or known military genius of his historical period. He was not ruthless or demanding, which put him at somewhat of a disadvantage when dealing with other leaders, both in the Christian and the Muslim camps. He did not build huge monuments to his own glory, and he spent years away from France, pursuing the Christian dream of the time.

Still Saint Louis IX stands as the model ruler because he brought a spiritual dimension to all sides of his life, including the use of unlimited power in ruling the nation, and a truly remarkable and beautiful sense of the faith — an element that glistened throughout his reign.

The central point of Louis's ambition was not power, not lands or wealth. Louis knew that such things would collapse and fade. He served Christ and that alone prompted his actions and his plans. He lived in the presence of God, a fact that transformed his personality and gave grace to his efforts.

Louis was very much a product of his own age, formed by the ideas of the time, the knowledge gathered by the scholars and the visions of the medieval artists. Events taking place around him molded him to some extent as well, but his deeply religious view of life itself served as a perspective that molded his ambitions for his own land. Because of this personal holiness, Louis IX was able to transcend, or rise above, the crude and ugly aspects of his own historical period, bringing new standards and new ideals into play.

He was born in a royal residence in Poissy, France, on April 25, 1214, the son of King Louis VIII and Queen Blanche. Blanche was originally from Castile, Spain, but she was part English as well, as the royal houses of the time intermarried in order to consolidate their powers. Blanche was a combination of such houses, possessing a considerable amount of personal strength and determination. The word formidable — something ferocious and unstoppable — could even be applied to Blanche, and probably was applied to her every day by those around her. France, however, was fortunate that this was so.

She raised Louis in a very Catholic household, being devout herself and used to having continuous religious services in the court. She was also a bright woman, quite capable of understanding national and international affairs, probably sitting with her husband as he heard reports from his ministers and agents. Blanche's quick mind and her innate (or natural) abilities to govern saved France when Louis VIII died in 1226, leaving an heir, Louis IX, who was only twelve years old.

Blanche became the regent and was forced to display all of her talents quickly. The enemies of the throne, outside of France and within its borders, were eager to test the queen's resolve and abilities. She made treaties, alliances, and even conducted wars in order to serve France's interest and to keep Louis's throne secure.

Louis studied daily and watched Blanche operate the royal administrative offices with skill. She also kept him on a very tight leash, as the saying goes, hoping to turn him into a monarch that would elevate France and the royal line from which he came. Certainly one did not have to look very far in those days to discover examples of what kings should *not* be. Blanche had studied them all, and she had intended from the start that Louis would be different.

Blanche even chose his wife for him, a woman named Margaret of Provence. That choice backfired on Blanche, who was taken quite by surprise when the royal couple met and lived together. Margaret married Louis in 1234, the year he ascended the throne. A sister-in-law of King Henry III of England, Margaret was also related to other royal houses in Europe.

Blanche had arranged the marriage for purely political reasons, and she was quite surprised to discover that the marriage turned into a genuine love match as well. Louis and Margaret went everywhere together, shared the same interests, laughed at one another's jokes even, and were both devout.

Love matches were not the usual relationships between the kings and queens of most countries at the time, and Blanche probably worried that this one would be a problem in time. The kings and queens of the lands did not date one another or fall in love before their weddings. Most queens arrived in a city at a very young age and married a total stranger, ready or not, for good or ill. Both partners, in fact, marched down the aisle and recited their wedding vows knowing that they were bound to their adopted royal husbands or wives without any hope of escape. Political alliances were the basis of these marriages, not romance.

Most kings and queens made the best of such arrangements, finding ways to develop what could be called alliances or truces. Some, however, hated one another at first sight and never did get used to wedlock, resulting in years of loneliness and a certain amount of pretense, meaning playacting or pretending. The playacting was necessary in public ceremonies. Kings and queens who had no use for each other had to smile and show affection for the sake of the people. Behind closed doors they argued constantly or developed techniques and routes through the palace that allowed them to avoid one another for days on end, resulting in temporary periods of peace. Now the offspring of such charming marriages often grew up a little odd. The kings and queens who appear strange or twisted may have been the products of such royal marriages, raised in an atmosphere of ugly rumors, dislike, even hatred.

Blanche had chosen Margaret in order to make Louis reasonably happy, but she did not expect that they would act like lovebirds in the court. She watched and tried to keep the lovers a bit distant, but Louis IX and Margaret found ways of being together.

They had eleven children. That was not unusual, considering the high death rate among infants at the time. Even the kings and queens trapped in truly unhappy marriages declared truces in order to provide the nation with much needed royal heirs. It was essential to have a son to follow on the throne because if a king or queen died without an heir, very often instability and wars were sure to follow. The nobles, always trying to figure out a way to win the throne for themselves, would have to choose a new king from among their ranks, but others might oppose their choice, plunging the realm into chaos and civil war. Years might follow during which the country would be torn apart by fighting and bloodshed. So bad could it become that the nation might be weakened, its strength sapped, its people starving and rebellious, and its borders no longer able to protect land and citizens from greedy neighbors. Every king and queen in the world was raised to know what might happen if royal couples did not set aside their differences and raise children for the protection of the throne.

Louis's coronation in 1234 sparked the usual amount of local rebellions, as inevitable as the cake at a wedding, especially when the newly crowned was young and not yet known in the battlefield. The nobles of France felt they could test the young king as they had his mother. It seems that many of the nobles believed that they had a personal right to the throne of the nation. Because so many families intermarried at the time, every noble could point to at least one uncle, cousin, or aunt who had royal blood. Using that relative, no matter how far removed or how distant in the past, the nobles rushed into battle to stake their claims whenever they thought they had a chance of toppling the present royal line.

These nobles found Louis as formidable as his mother and swiftly retreated. The king was not responding only to the threat of a noble uprising. He fought with severity and harshness because he understood absolute power. France would be destroyed if some of the aristocrats were left to their own ambitions. They cared nothing for the people. Their goal was absolute power, but they came badly equipped to handle it successfully. Blanche had instilled a powerful sense of might and right in her son, and those who crossed his path with evil intent found themselves facing a very ferocious individual.

Once the nobles were put into retreat, Louis started his reign in peace. That peace was soon to be broken, however, as Henry III of England, Queen Margaret's brother-in-law, began an assault on French cities along the coast. For centuries England and France battled over such towns, since both claimed the region as originally part of their own realms, or empires. Louis defeated the English army at a place called Taillebourg in 1242, ending the threat. He then conducted other campaigns to gain new lands and to tighten his hold on those already under his control. When he completed this task, France was secure and prosperous.

The main task confronting him at that stage was France itself. He turned his attention to conditions within his own kingdom, bringing a new spirit to his people as he reformed the government wherever possible. Under the regulations and laws that he introduced and strictly enforced, vassals were protected by certain rights. Vassals were peasants, or serfs, who were quite literally chained to the land in noble estates. Born into a village, such men and women were forbidden in most cases to move and they had to perform whatever tasks their lords set for them.

Louis reined in the nobles, having the advantage of having beaten many of them on the battlefield soon after his coronation. He enforced the rules making such nobles responsible for the care of their vassals, something that sounded quite revolutionary in that day and age. He also limited the amount of taxes and work that a noble could demand from the commoners on his estates. That regulation, of course, almost gave the nobles heart attacks. Many of them lived well because they could drain their peasants dry without fearing any retribution, or punishment. If they were unpopular with their own peasants, they did not care. Many traveled their own lands with bodyguards, veterans of wars who could protect them against any peasant crazy enough to try to take revenge for past abuses.

Louis also introduced Roman law into many areas of his government, regulating the legal systems and providing the average man and woman with some protection in the French courts. Before these laws were enacted the peasants were brutally punished for minor crimes, such as stealing a piece of bread, walking in forests set aside by nobles for their hunting, or even getting in the way of a noble while he was riding on a road. These ancient laws shook up France and gave new hope to the common people, who thought that at last they might prosper a bit on their own.

As a result of such legal measures, Louis was earning a reputation for his just and sensible decisions. Even though he was young, he was asked to settle disputes in other lands. He was regarded as a brilliant man, pious, honest, and willing to do whatever was necessary for the common good.

He had another desire, however, a deep longing that would lead him halfway across the known world, an ambition nurtured by the Christian faith and by the temper of the times. Louis wanted to fulfill yet another obligation of the Christian kings of the era, and for this reason he decided to embark upon a crusade to the Holy Land to help free Jerusalem from the Muslims. The crusades had been ongoing since 1095 but had thus far yielded little results, despite the efforts of thousands of knights and soldiers, the deaths of simple but devout souls, and the best efforts of many kings. Jerusalem, the holy city, had been captured during the First Crusade, but it later fell to the armies of the Muslims, especially under the famous general named Saladin. The crusaders had not fared well for many years in the Holy Land, losing ground and holdings there steadily in the face of hard and determined Islamic troops who matched the Christian fervor (or enthusiasm) with one of their own.

For Louis, the crusade was an obligation that he had to fulfill if he was to call himself a true Christian monarch. In the thinking of that time, one proved devotion and faithfulness by going on a crusade, even if it had little chance of succeeding. Many other rulers found ways to avoid setting out, preferring to stay at home rather than take an army that was expensive and difficult to keep halfway around the world.

Such an attitude makes sense to modern people; but during the Middle Ages, this sort of behavior was considered cowardly and most unchivalrous, meaning it went against the strict codes of knightly honor by which all kings and warriors lived. Louis was a knight, and a Christian. He had to fulfill this last kingly obligation or die in the attempt.

Now, looking back, it might seem strange that a saint should be willing to march off to war, knowing that human beings would die in far-off battlefields. Again, one must remember the way people thought during the Middle Ages. The crusade was called a holy war, a struggle to free sacred places from the occupation of what were called infidels — people who were enemies of one's faith. Europeans were taught that it was a good thing to go and kill Muslims, an idea that seems very offensive today, even though such wars are still going on in the world. King Louis did not plan just to massacre infidels; instead, he saw the war as a necessary evil, a conflict that had to be fought for the good of Christendom. Honorable, chivalrous, and sincere that he was doing the right thing, Louis is revered as a saint not because he went to war but because of his abiding faith and goodness. The times in which he lived taught that spilling blood on behalf of the Holy Land was an expression of devotion and belief.

Louis, convinced and bound by honor to go, consulted experts and asked them what the best destination would be in the Holy Land. These so-called experts, most of them veterans of past crusades, talked among themselves and declared that the most suitable place to attack was not Palestine but Egypt. They claimed that Egypt could be captured and then the crusader army could march north and conquer the Holy Land without having to risk being cut off from much needed supplies.

Unfortunately, this was very bad advice, as time would prove. In 1249, Louis sailed with a French army into the Mediterranean, landing at Damietta, a site in the delta of the great Nile River, the waterway that streams more than four thousand miles out of the heart of Africa, north to the Mediterranean Sea. The people living in the area, of course, could not believe their eyes when they saw the fleet coming into the harbor area. Some ran to mosques to pray, while others headed toward the great Muslim strongholds to alert their allies there.

Thus began what was called the Seventh Crusade, one of the last such efforts ever launched by Christian Europe. Surrounded by sand, undrinkable water, swamps, and the blazing heat, the knights were suddenly confronted as well by an army of Muslims, called Saracens by the crusaders. The Saracens were excellent fighters, swarming over the hot, thirsty, and hungry Christian forces. The battle was fierce, ending finally with the total defeat of the knights.

Louis was captured by the enemy and, in the custom of the time, was held for ransom. The queen mother, Blanche, collected the money and sent a huge treasure of eight hundred thousand gold pieces to win her son's freedom — a really true king's ransom at that time or even now. Freed from an Islamic dungeon with a fellow prisoner, a writer named Jean de Joinville, Louis did not return to France. Instead, he went to the Christian fortress of Acre, on the Palestinian coast, a mighty castle held by knights. It would, in fact, be the last possession of the crusaders to fall in the Holy Land, in 1291.

Just why Louis did not return home is open to speculation, or possible interpretation. At Acre he was in the company of knights and warriors and in the spiritual care of priests. Louis remained in the fortress until 1254, returning to France only after the death of his "formidable" mother. He may have also spent the time at Acre trying to find allies and friends who might help him return to the field. He still harbored hopes of capturing Jerusalem, an ambition that would have fateful consequences.

A book written about Louis by Jean de Joinville, by now a close friend in good times and bad, describes the saint in this period. Jean depicts Louis as generous of spirit, brave, full of common sense, yet filled with genuine piety and holy zeal. All of these virtues would shine once Louis returned to France.

In 1259, Louis conducted the Treaty of Paris, ending his feud with King Henry III of England. He also rebuilt the beautiful church of Sainte-Chapelle in Paris. In this small but stunning church Louis placed a special relic that had been given to him by another ruler. The relic was said to be the crown of thorns, the same crown worn by our Lord during his passion, when he was whipped by the Romans just before his crucifixion. Sadly, the crown of thorns was taken from Sainte-Chapelle during the French Revolution in the late 1700s and probably destroyed, only one of the many outrages committed against the Church in France by the mobs of nonbelievers. Elsewhere, Paris was beautified by an ambitious building program that made it one of the envies of the West. With his attentions so focused, Louis helped forge a time of peace and prosperity for his kingdom, a type of renewal that had not been known for many years.

In affairs of national defense, Louis built up the French navy and saw a true flowering of the Gothic style of architecture throughout the land. There was peace on the frontiers, the crops were bountiful, nobles content, and the economy prospering. It was indeed a kind of Golden Age.

Louis was also a mighty patron of the religious orders who had come recently to the city of Paris, namely the so-called mendicant orders, the Franciscans and Dominicans. The name mendicant meant that they lived entirely through the charity of others, holding no wealth or property. Both orders were seen by Louis as very helpful in strengthening the faith and in advancing the teachings of the Church. As a result of his patronage (or high favor) of the Dominicans in Paris, King Louis showed his pleasure at the work of one friar in particular. This was Saint Thomas Aquinas, whom the Church reveres as one of its greatest thinkers.

The king sent out invitations for the Dominicans to dine with him in his palace. The friars knew enough not to decline a royal invitation, even though they were reluctant to leave their simple monasteries for the luxurious halls of the king. Louis made them more than welcome. He spoke to them about many things, including the faith, for the king was well educated, able to converse freely on many complex theological subjects.

Thomas Aquinas was always especially hesitant about going to dine with King Louis. He much preferred to stay at home and work, pray, and think. One evening, in fact, his habit of sitting and devoting his whole mind to his work caused a humorous incident. Thomas was at the royal table, but he paid little attention to the king's conversation, thinking instead about some theological problem. Suddenly the answer came to him, and he pounded on the royal table, shouting out in triumph. All conversation stopped as courtiers were shocked that someone had dared to cry out in front of the king! Thomas realized what he had done. Rising from his chair, he bowed to the king and apologized for his rudeness, explaining that he had just solved an important matter of theology. Instead of being angry, Louis merely smiled. Knowing the importance of Thomas's work for the Church, he dismissed the apology of the friar and commanded that scribes should come immediately and take down the dictation of Thomas so that there was no chance that the thoughts of the great Dominican might be forgotten. Here was a king who ruled with grace and lived like a Christian.

He accomplished all that he had dreamed for France, but the conquest of the Holy Land remained out of his reach. The sacred places had not lost their allure, calling to Louis like a treasure in the desert. He also heard the cries of the Christian prisoners and slaves, men and women taken by the Muslims and held in bondage.

Convinced to take up the holy cross of Christ one more time, Louis embarked on the Eighth Crusade in 1270, leaving France forever. Before he sailed away, he gave his son a book called *Testament*, in which he stated all that he believed was right and true for monarchs, or kings. That remarkable document shows Louis's spirit and his wisdom concerning power and the obligations of the thrones of the world.

Once again Louis sailed on a holy quest, landing in North Africa near the ancient city of Carthage. This spot had been chosen as a result of a clever scheme of the Muslims. It seems that the Islamic rulers in Egypt and Africa learned that another crusader invasion was imminent (or soon to take place). Fearing that they might actually lose to the French king, they hatched a plot to misdirect him and his army.

A message was sent to Louis from a local potentate (or ruler) in Tunis, an official called a bey. He made some rather obscure promises to aid Louis in his war, and even gave hints that he would consider becoming a Christian. This was enough for Louis, who lived by his word and understood honor as a vital aspect of the role of a ruler. He believed the bey and accepted his offer.

French troops landed at Carthage and set out for Tunis. It was only then that Louis learned of his predicament, or difficult situation. The bey had only pretended to offer his aid. Louis and his knights were stranded in the middle of a terrible desert, miles from reinforcements and running out of food and water. Matters only became worse when a disease, typhus, broke out in his camp. The king caught the disease, collapsing in the arms of his loyal knights. On August 25, 1270, King Louis died in his tent. The crusade was over, his dream of saving Jerusalem for the Christian faith never realized.

From the time of his death, Louis was honored as a saintly figure. He stood as a symbol of honor and chivalry, as well as prayerful devotion and all of the Christian virtues. It was not very long before miracles were reported and his name was considered worthy of possible canonization. In 1297, only twenty-seven years after his death, King Louis was canonized by Pope Boniface VIII and declared the patron of the French kings. Because of his other labors during his lifetime, he was honored as the patron of soldiers, stone masons, and sculptors. His work still stands throughout Paris, the city he loved. His feast day is August 25.

Lucy de Freitas

Chapter 14

Lucy de Freitas

A Catholic statement written at the start of this century says: "There is not in the whole history of the Church a single people who can offer to the admiration of the Christian world annals as glorious and a martyrology as lengthy as those of the people of Japan."

Even though Saint Paul Miki and his Japanese companions have been raised to the altars of the Church, few Catholics around the world understand the rich tapestry of faith that has been woven over the centuries in that nation. Saint Francis Xavier arrived in the Japanese islands in 1549, converting around two thousand during his brief stay and starting the great Catholic tradition that continues into modern times.

Other missionary priests followed Francis Xavier, and the Church became part of the Japanese scene in a time filled with much unrest and violence. Long wars conducted by the ruling clans of Japan had left the country divided and troubled. Feuds and battles ravaged the various provinces, and more and more people looked to their nobles for some sign of unity and central authority that would halt the destruction and suffering.

Three men would rise in this time of Japan's political and social upheaval. Samurai, warriors trained in the military code of honor that ruled the lives of the nation's great families or clans, these three men would not only bring Japan into an era of unity and peace but would also have a lasting effect on the Church and on the devout Catholics of the various Japanese islands.

The first to begin the long battle-racked journey toward a unified Japan was Oda Nobunaga, the heir to a famous dynasty that dated back centuries in the land. Nobunaga, the heir to the Oda line, was only fifteen years old when his father died. He immediately went to war to protect his holdings, even taking the acting shogun, the administrator of Japan for the emperor, as a political captive.

Oda Nobunaga, addressed in that fashion because the Japanese style of writing a name places the clan title first, counted among his military strategists and generals a talented individual who was a convert to the Church. Impressed with the skills and the spirit of this man, Oda Nobunaga looked upon the Catholic missionaries with tolerance, having benefited from their training in the person of his adviser. There were an estimated two hundred thousand Catholics in Japan during this period, and two hundred fifty churches served the needs of the growing number of converts. Having the patronage of Oda Nobunaga allowed the Church to flourish, because few of the other Japanese clan lords wanted to cross swords with him, especially over religious affairs.

Oda Nobunaga, however, was slain in a surprise attack in 1582, and his patronage of the Church ended with his passing. He was only forty-eight when he was killed, but he had put an end to Japan's civil wars and had started the reorganization of the government to better conditions for the common people in the various provinces.

Following Oda Nobunaga was Toyotomi Hideyoshi, a gifted man called "Monkey." This remarkable commoner had served the Oda clan and had been given the family name of Toyotomi when he had risen to a high degree of power. When he followed Oda Nobunaga as the administrator of Japan, he did not receive the title of shogun because of his commoner background, because he did not belong to the traditional clan that held filled that role, and because he had no ancestral right to the rank. The lack of a proper title did not stop Hideyoshi from keeping a tight rein on other clans. He had been trained by Oda Nobunaga, was just as ruthless in putting down his opponents, and shared the same vision of a unified nation and a central government that could keep the peace assured.

Some of the great noble houses of Japan were already Catholic by the time Hideyoshi took over control of the islands. When Pope Sixtus V was installed in Rome in 1585, the samurai lords of Bungo, Arima, and Omura sent envoys to witness the ceremonies. These Japanese received papal honors in return. Date Masamune, one of Japan's most honored warriors, the lord of Sendai, was also a Catholic. He sent a legate (or representative), Asakura Roku-yemon, to visit Pope Paul V and the king of Spain.

Aware of the widespread Catholic influence, Hideyoshi maintained a policy of quiet toleration at first, although some lords of various provinces conducted campaigns of harassment against their local Catholics. In 1560, for example, one lord demanded that the Catholics in his province abandon the faith. Rather than surrender their beliefs, these faithful abandoned their homes and fortunes and fled to the region called Bungo, where they lived in poverty but in peace.

Three Spanish Franciscan priests were welcomed in Hideyoshi's court in 1593, despite the growing concern of many about the presence of so many Europeans in the country. Many feared the Europeans, believing that they would arrive in vast numbers one day to make Japan a colonial province. The Japanese could look all across the world to see the sort of violent behavior toward local populations by many gold-hungry Westerners. Their fears about the Europeans were based on hard facts and reality. Hideyoshi listened to them, but he stayed neutral where the Church was concerned and allowed the convert programs to continue without official hindrances.

Then a disastrous event took place, a classic case of human stupidity and European arrogance. As a result, the Japanese policy was altered abruptly and cruelly. Thousands would perish because of one man's idiocy; martyrs would suffer because of one man's pride.

A Spanish ship, the *San Felipe*, ran aground on the Japanese coast during Hideyoshi's reign. As Japanese officials came on board to investigate the accident and to set about freeing the vessel, the captain of the ship conducted himself with rudeness and no sense of Japanese scholarship and linguistic skills. Above all, the captain did not understand the Japanese code of honor or the extent to which the circumstances of life would be changed to meet that code. Coming face to face with the Japanese officials on the deck of his ship, the captain was probably a bit unnerved. These warriors could appear ferocious and dangerous. Perhaps without thinking, he actually made the comment that he was happy that all Catholic missionaries in Japan were just the start of a European invasion.

There was no such invasion planned, and the man was certainly not a high-ranked individual who would be in on any future military adventure being planned by the crowned heads of Europe. Seeing the Japanese officials, he started showing off to his crewmen, making fun of the native people so that he would look good by comparison. He also stupidly spoke about the "invasion" in Spanish, not realizing that the Japanese had learned his language, along with Dutch, English, and Portuguese. The Japanese gave no sign that they heard the captain, and they went about their business with their usual efficiency. He sailed away, not realizing that he had dropped a bomb on the Catholic missions and had condemned countless souls to torment at the hands of the Japanese authorities.

Needless to say, it was not very long before Hideyoshi heard about the Spanish captain's words. They served to back up all of the complaints being made about the Europeans, and they fanned the fires of suspicion and hatred against the Church. Hideyoshi was dumbfounded when he heard the report and the captain's claims. They forced him into an activity that he had formerly shunned but one that was now deemed necessary. Fearing the threat of foreigners who had no regard for Japanese customs or traditions, and moving to safeguard his land and his people from further contamination, Hideyoshi declared war on the Church.

Catholic priests were arrested in December of 1596, and Christians in various key locations were tracked down and listed in government records for future campaigns. On February 5, 1597, twenty-six Catholics were crucified in the city of Nagasaki. They died singing hymns and giving praise to God. Among the martyrs were a thirteen-year-old and a twelve-year-old. So joyfully did these martyrs accept their fate that their executioners and observers were struck dumb with astonishment. The Catholics died with the same ferocity and honor as the samurai of old.

Hideyoshi died in 1598, leaving a young son by a second wife as his heir. The lad, despite the schemes and courage of his mother, would never live to take true power. He faced the most formidable foe possible, one that could not afford to allow the lad to gain Hideyoshi's power. The third samurai lord was now free to take control of the nation.

His name was Tokugawa Ieyasu and, besides laying ancestral claim to the shogunate, he had one of the most brilliant minds in Japan at the time. Brave, cunning in battle, and holding a vision of a unified Japan, this noble was able to survive the reigns of Oda Nobunaga and Hideyoshi. He was also able to inspire the hearts and minds of many in the clans, building an army that could defeat anyone crazy enough to come against him.

As a young lad of twelve, Ieyasu had put on the samurai armor. He was a military genius and the sort of lord that attracted allies and companions. Oda Nobunaga, at first an enemy, became his patron, instilling in him the vision of a Japan freed from clan feuds and wars. Ieyasu had also learned to crush potential enemies without mercy and with a speed that left onlookers breathless.

He met the claims of Hideyoshi's heir almost instantly, at first safeguarding the lad and then responding to the ambitions of the Hideyoshi clan as they became more and more evident. When Ieyasu destroyed Osaka Castle, the home of Hideyoshi's son and heir, he reigned supreme in the land. This victory prompted the Japanese to state: "Oda Nobunaga planted the wheat. Hideyoshi harvested the wheat. Ieyasu enjoys the bread."

For about fifteen years after becoming shogun, this warrior did not hinder the Church, as he was busy consolidating (or strengthening and making more solid) his position by bringing the last rebellious clans in the distant provinces into line. Ieyasu was also making plans for a new capital at a place called Edo, or Yedo, now modern Tokyo.

During the peace, one hundred thirty Jesuits, as well as Franciscans, Dominicans, and Augustinians, arrived in Japan and went about their missionary labors without any difficulties. In 1614, however, Tokugawa Ieyasu, the undisputed shogun, announced that Catholicism would no longer be tolerated in any region of Japan. All traces of the Church were to be abolished. As a result, persecutions began immediately, a practice that his son, Shogun Tokugawa Hidetoda, maintained when he came to power at the death of Ieyasu.

The "Great Martyrdom" took place on September 10, 1622, at Nagasaki, and an eighty-year-old woman named Lucy de Freitas was among the victims of this persecution. She was Japanese, and a widow, having married a Portuguese merchant named Felipe de Freitas, becoming a Catholic of incredible zeal. She adopted her Christian name with pride and served the Church faithfully each day of her life. She visited hospitals, cared for the needy, and led local Rosary groups in the city. Even though she was quite frail and elderly when the persecution began, she was absolutely fearless.

Lucy was a Third Order Franciscan, belonging to the religious community of laypersons who shared in the rich spiritual tradition begun by Saint Francis of Assisi. The *Poverello*, the "Little Poor Man," as Francis was called, served as her model, and she tried to practice all of his virtues. As part of her Franciscan obligation, Lucy offered shelter to a Franciscan priest named Blessed Richard of Saint Anne. She knew that an apostate (someone who had given up the faith and denied Christ) was watching her activities and reporting them to the authorities, but she did not let that stop her from giving shelter to the Franciscan.

She was promptly arrested and tried for harboring a priest, which was a very severe offense under the law. Lucy was ordered to denounce the faith in order to save her life. She refused and spoke so eloquently about Christ that the judge became extremely angry. He ordered her silenced and then condemned her to death by fire as punishment for her zeal. Most Christian women were decapitated, or beheaded (meaning they had their heads cut off); but Lucy was burned at the stake, joining twenty-two other martyrs who were also put to the torch. Before they died in the flames, they watched the beheading of twenty-nine fellow Christians. All of them died with prayers on their lips, praising God. The Japanese believed that was the end of Lucy de Freitas, but they were wrong, as the Romans and countless others had erred in the past when dealing with the Church and the martyrs. Revered in a special way, Lucy de Freitas was beatified in 1867, along with her companions.

She was not the last Japanese who would face a grim death in the name of Christ. In 1624, there were two hundred eighty-five Catholics martyred during a period of three months. Hundreds more perished in 1627, again filling the place of execution with praise and joy.

An eyewitness to one of the ceremonies of martyrdom was an English sea captain named Richard Cocks. He came away from the executions quite awe-struck and filled with admiration for the martyrs. Captain Cocks stated that he watched fifty-five Japanese Catholics die in Kyoto. He said that small children were in the center of rings of flames, held in their mothers' arms. As they were dying, the children cried out, "Jesus, receive our souls!"

Hoping to find refuge and safety, Christians took control of the fortress of Shimabara in 1637. From the castle, the Christians tried to negotiate with the government, but the shogun would not listen. An army attacked the walls, and thousands died with honor, reminding their executioners of the samurai who had long faced death with dignity and pride.

In 1640, four ambassadors from Portugal were arrested and

commanded to deny their faith. When they refused, they were slain; their diplomatic status did not protect them from death. A stern edict had been issued in Japan, stating:

While the sun warms the earth,
let no Christian be so bold as
to venture into Japan. Let
this be known to all men.
Though it were the King of Spain
in person or the God of the
Christians . . . whosoever
shall disobey this prohibition
will pay for it with his head.

The edict and the martyrdoms sprang from a deep-rooted need for isolation among the Japanese people in that era. Watching the Europeans, the Japanese admired their technical skills and their inventions but were shocked and disgusted by many other characteristics displayed, especially by the European sailors. Such men, drunken, disorderly, and covered with filth (such Europeans did not bathe very often), disturbed the Japanese because they represented disorder. The Shinto and Buddhist religions were part of the Japanese culture, whereas Catholicism was totally Westernized, introducing a foreign way of life into society. It was probably for these reasons that the Church was singled out for destruction. The Catholic faith also provided its members with a code of honor and a zeal that matched the samurai traditions of the old clan families. The martyrs in their joyous deaths only confirmed this aspect of the faith, renewing the shogun's attempts to eradicate all of its influences.

Blessed Lucy de Freitas and her companions did not die in vain. In 1865, when Japan opened to Commodore Perry and his American warships, Catholics welcomed the Westerners to Japan. It is believed that as many as fifty thousand Catholics remained true to the faith. They learned to stay hidden while they nurtured their children in the love of Christ. Today, the Church is very much alive in Japan, thriving and secure because of those, like Lucy de Freitas, who walked into the fire of martyrdom centuries ago.

Chapter 15

Martha

Sometimes the people who work the hardest are the ones who receive the least amount of appreciation or thanks, especially from their own relatives. They become invisible to other family members, working alone and without recognition. For instance, every day members of families go to their kitchen or dining-room tables knowing that nutritious, good-tasting meals will be waiting for them. They take such meals for granted, not giving a single thought to the time and energy involved in their preparation. These family members would die of shock if the meals they relied upon were not waiting on the table at breakfast, lunch, or dinner, but it never dawns on them to thank the cook of the household or to express their satisfaction. Most sit down, eat as fast as they can, and then disappear from the room without a word.

Saint Martha was very much the one in her family who was frequently overlooked, at least as far as it appears from the Gospel accounts. She has not been forgotten by the Church, however, and her life remains a strange and wonderful example of serving God wherever he places one, in all types of climates and circumstances.

She was the chief cook and bottle washer of a rather large house in the small community known as Bethany; at least she supervised all of the preparations and cleaning for the household. People who lived in Bethany, which was a suburb of Jerusalem (now in modern Israel), were not too poor to have servants. Martha was the sister of a woman named Mary and a man called Lazarus. Yes, this was the Lazarus raised from the dead by Jesus.

Probably the oldest of the three, Martha had no doubt been placed in charge of the household when their mother died and remained in that position ever after. Many women, even in this day and age, inherit the responsibilities of looking after large families because they are the firstborn. Most of them learned housekeeping at their mother's knee, knowing that they would be expected to take over such a role in due time.

They put their own personal dreams and ambitions on hold so that younger brothers and sisters can receive the care they need. These women watch the younger ones complete their education and go on to fine jobs or good marriages, and eventually they discover that they are alone, forgotten by the relatives they raised with such devotion.

Martha, fortunately, was not alone in her big house. She and Mary and Lazarus lived together obviously content to make their way while watching the world go by. The world passing just in front of their doorstep, given their closeness to Jerusalem, was a pretty interesting place. Bethany, after all, was less than two miles from Jerusalem, on the edge of the Judaean Desert and built on the slope of the Mount of Olives, a location that provided them with a great view of their world.

Now Jesus visited Bethany, being a close friend of the family. He certainly was there on his way to Jerusalem, as we shall see, believed by many scholars as making his triumphant entrance into Jerusalem from Bethany on Palm Sunday. He would even come back there after his resurrection, bringing his disciples with him, as was reported in the Gospel of Saint Luke.

But Jesus was not the only notable personage to go past the doors of the house of Martha. At Jerusalem during the time of Jesus' entry into the holy city were King Herod Antipas and Pontius Pilate, the Roman official called a procurator who had charge over all of Judaea.

Herod Antipas was tetrarch, or ruler, over two small territories called Galilee and Perea. A son of the infamous King Herod the Great (who had slain all the infants in Bethlehem in the hopes of killing the newborn Messiah), Herod Antipas lived most of the time in one of two places. The first was a city called Tiberias, which served as the capitol city of his kingdom, and the second was Jerusalem.

Tiberias was not a popular place among the Jews because it had originally been built on an ancient cemetery associated with the ruined city once called Hammath. Now the Jews believed that a city built on top of a cemetery was unclean. Only crazy people went to live in such a place, and certainly Jews who practiced their religion wanted no part of such a site. Herod Antipas, who had largely created Tiberias in honor of the Roman emperor Tiberius, did not much consider such traditions. He sent out invitations to his people to move into the new and beautiful city, scratching his head in disappointment when no one took up his offer. Refusing to give up, he established a population in the city by sending out his soldiers on well-disciplined raids. They returned with people at sword- and spear-point who were forced to live in Tiberias. Troops stationed at the gates and patrolling the streets made certain that no one tried to escape to healthier destinations.

Needless to say, this sort of treatment, well known everywhere because people carried the tales of the enforced residences, made Herod quite unpopular with the Jews. He did not help his cause by choosing a wife for himself after a time. One of Herod's brothers, called Philip, who lived in Rome, was married to a woman named Herodias. Deciding that Herod Antipas was someone destined to gain power and prestige, Herodias divorced Philip, married Herod, and moved into the palace at Tiberias, bringing with her a daughter, Salome.

If the Jewish people thought Herod Antipas was out of his head when he built a city over a cemetery, they were struck speechless by the marriage. This sort of thing just was not done by anyone who understood Jewish teachings. The marriage was considered a grievous sin to the Jews, and Herod was loudly criticized. One of the loudest voices was that of Saint John the Baptist. So troublesome did the Baptist become, in fact, that Herod had him arrested and thrown into a dungeon. Herodias was especially angry at the Baptist because of his nonstop condemning of her marriage and her sinful life. Herodias, of course, hatched the terrible plot that resulted in John's execution by Herod and the giving of his head to Salome as a gift after she had performed a dance. Handing the head of John the Baptist to Salome on a silver platter did nothing for Herod's cause. He was despised for this murder. The priests of Jerusalem might not have understood the Baptist, but they gave him credit for being a prophet. Jewish kings did not go around beheading prophets.

When Herod resided in Jerusalem throughout part of the year, especially at times of important Jewish festivals, he was shunned by many as a result of his crimes and his disregard of Jewish law. He was in the holy city at the time of the Passover and so was on hand to receive a special prisoner sent to him by the Romans. The prisoner was Christ, and Herod played his part in the dramatic events leading to the death of the Lord on the cross.

Herodias would learn before too long that she had divorced, schemed, and plotted for nothing, because Herod would fall from power. Stripped of his throne by the Emperor Caligula for conspiring against Rome, Herod and his wife were exiled to Gaul (modern France), where they died in obscurity (meaning they had been forgotten).

The other person of importance in Jerusalem was Pontius Pilate, the Roman procurator. A governor of the region, Pontius Pilate had responsibility over Judaea (the area in which many Jews lived and which controlled Jerusalem), but he was answerable to a higher-ranked official, the powerful governor of Syria, which was one of Rome's most important possessions in all of the empire.

The procurator and his troops were stationed in the building called the Antonia Fortress in the heart of Jerusalem. The fort was naturally shunned by the Jews because it was a symbol of the Roman occupation of their land and because it was the place where the Romans kept their pagan idols and battle standards. Pilate, who conducted the trial of Jesus, never got on well with the Jews. If a delegation of Jewish leaders came to meet with him, he had to step outside of the Antonia Fortress to greet them or go without seeing them at all because they refused to enter. When he tried to build an aqueduct (a way of bringing water into the city), he used temple money to pay for the project, a rather stupid error on his part. This was so horrifying to the Jews that they promptly rioted, and Pilate's troops ended up killing many of them, something considered really bad form by the Romans.

Philo of Alexandria, a writer of the era, declared that Pilate was a man who resorted to "briberies, violence, robberies, wanton injustices, executions without trials . . . and ceaseless and supremely grievous cruelty." That sort of reputation finally caught up with the procurator. He was recalled to Rome by Emperor Tiberius to stand trial for various crimes. Pilate arrived there in time to see Tiberius being laid to rest and crazy Emperor Caligula on the throne.

Whatever happened to Pontius Pilate at the hands of Caligula is not known with certainty. Pilate supposedly threw himself off one of the mountains in the Alps, but that is only one tradition. Another version of his attempts at suicide includes a tale of how he jumped into the Tiber River in Rome, planning to drown himself. The Tiber, however, made a loud noise — like it tasted something terrible — and threw Pilate back onto the shore, wanting nothing further to do with the executioner of the Savior.

Pilate, Herod Antipas, and countless others moved in and out of Jerusalem, and Martha and her family witnessed the processions. As we have seen, Christ was one of their visitors on occasion, as the hospitality of the home was well known by the followers of Jesus. Whenever he was in the house, Martha fussed over his meals and made sure that everything was clean and comfortable.

Her sister, Mary, it appears, just sat at Christ's feet, not lifting a finger to help out with the household chores. Martha, of course, put up with that for about an hour or two, but the house was filled with guests and there was just too much to do to keep everyone comfortable. Urging Mary to help her and finding herself ignored, Martha finally complained to Jesus, who turned to tell her: "It is Mary who has the better part."

Now this sounds like a real put-down — what could be called a stinging rebuke. Scholars believe that Jesus was telling Martha and future generations of Christians that Mary, her sister, represented those who put aside all else for his sake. It is good to be busy about many things in the service of the Church, but one has to remember Christ as the center of everything. When he came into the house, Mary forgot about meals and clean clothes. No one recorded how Martha felt about being told such a thing, but she apparently continued to work and to serve everyone with the same generous spirit of hospitality.

It was Martha, not Mary, however, who came to meet Jesus and the Apostles after the death of Lazarus. Mary was too upset to welcome the Savior according to the historical accounts. Martha made the effort, saying that if Jesus had been with her brother, Lazarus would not have died. She said this openly to Christ, and he rewarded her faith by summoning Lazarus out of the grave.

Some scholars believe that Veronica, the woman who supposedly stopped the procession of Jesus and the soldiers on the way to Calvary, was Martha. (We will discuss Veronica in the last chapter of this book.) The name Veronica was taken from the Latin for *vera icon*, the "true image." There is no documentation or actual reference to Martha, but it rings true in a way. She would have been concerned about Jesus, and a few Roman soldiers would not have bothered her much.

Martha, Mary, and Lazarus did not abandon the Apostles or Christ after the ascension of the Lord and Pentecost. They played a part in the birth of the Church and the in the life of the young Christian community. Like many of the other Apostles and figures of the early Church, the three were mentioned in legends and tales in several places, none of which have been proven as fact.

One has them traveling to Gaul, or modern France, where they helped to preach the Gospel to the inhabitants. Martha's relics, in fact, were discovered in the city of Tarascon, in Provence, France, in 1187.

In portraits, she is shown with a set of keys, the symbol of the housekeeper. She is also shown holding a broom and a ladle. Sometimes Saint Martha is depicted with a dragon at her side, a reference to an obscure legend from France. According to this, Martha once killed a dragon. This probably seems pretty weird, that a saint other than George should be honored as a dragon slayer, but several are portrayed as having dragons at their feet. One has to remember the images used by the everyday, common people in the Middle Ages. The dragon was a mighty sign of evil and wickedness. When a saint was shown as having slain a dragon, it meant that this holy person had triumphed over sin and evil. It was supposed to give encouragement to the simple folk who were wrestling, not with fire-breathing, wing-flapping dragons, but with their own sinful natures.

In Martha's case, she was said to have met a terrible dragon named Tarasque at the town of Aix-la-Chapelle. With the help of the Lord, she managed to slay the dragon and so save the town from its brutal mastery. Martha is actually not the only saint so honored. In fact, aside from Saint George, other saints who have supposedly slain dragons were Margaret, Philip, and Michael the Archangel, as well as really obscure saints such as Florent, Clement of Metz, and Romain of Rouen, who was honored as the slayer of a nasty dragon named La Gargouille (or "The Gargoyle").

Saint Martha is also the patron of cooks, servants, and innkeepers. Her feast day is July 29.

Martin of Tours

Chapter 16

Martin of Tours

In the year 337, at the gates of the city of Amiens, in modern France, a young soldier came across a feeble, half-naked man who was clearly suffering in the bitter cold of the season. Without a second thought, the soldier took his sword and cut his military cloak in half. He wrapped the woolen material around the beggar, warming him, and then went on his way.

That night, however, the soldier had a vision in a dream, one that would change his life forever and would help thousands in their search for the truth of the faith. In the vision, Christ stood before him, wrapped in the part of the cloak that he had given to the beggar. The young soldier was Saint Martin of Tours, one of the great bishops of his age and a remarkable man with stamina, unbridled energy, and a certain brilliance of mind.

He was born around 316 in a place called Sabaria, that city being part of the Roman Empire in an area that would eventually become modern Hungary. His family was stationed there because his father was an officer in the Roman army and had been assigned by his superiors to the garrison of that city. The family was pagan, believing in the old gods of Rome, but Martin knew about Christianity and agreed in his heart with what he heard about that religion. The Church was spreading rapidly at that time because of Emperor Constantine and continued imperial favor, which halted persecutions in all of the provinces.

When Martin's father was assigned to an army post in Pavia (in what is now Italy), the family made the long journey to start a new home there, knowing such hardships and relocations were part of the military life. Martin was not allowed to enjoy his new home for long, however, as he had turned fifteen, the age at which boys were eligible for military service, ready or not, willing or not. He became a soldier because that was the law, and he marched with his regiment to Amiens in Gaul (now modern France).

It was there that he met the beggar, and it was there that he had his vision of Christ. The vision naturally distracted him and made him question the paths of his life. Martin was probably not terribly enthusiastic about military life. In those days especially, a man had to be born to the battlefield, had to like drills and marches and hand-to-hand combat. Most of the regular soldiers didn't live very long; but those who did, gained rewards on their retirement.

As a result of the vision, which prompted a great deal of soul-searching on Martin's part (and probably causing him to admit his dislike of the military service), he began a campaign to get himself honorably discharged from the army. It took a while, because the request was considered odd, and he was in the Rhine River region when he received his discharge, having marched there with his unit. Romans in service at the time could expect to see the world, because the various legion units were rotated and sent where needed.

Upon being discharged, he went immediately to the city of Poitiers, where the bishop, Saint Hilary, was training converts and winning fervent souls to Christ. Martin was baptized in Hilary's cathedral, and then he made the long journey homeward to see his family. Upon arriving home, he was startled to learn that members of the Arian heresy, a group opposing traditional Catholic teaching and the pontiff, were now in control of that area in the roles of high-placed churchmen. As Martin spoke out against Arian ideas, which he viewed as dangerous nonsense, he became a marked man among those in charge.

He was finally forced to leave his family, some of whom he had converted, and to flee from the Arian stronghold. Along the way he discovered that Hilary had been forced from Poitiers by other Arians, a fact that dismayed him and made him look for a spiritual refuge where he could once again sort out things in his own heart and mind.

Now it sounds weird that Catholics were persecuting other Catholics for following the pope and the Church's traditional teachings. The Arians were just another brand of heretics, and they soon discovered the sad truth that people who teach error may have the upper hand in the Church for a time; but they are doomed inevitably as reason and grace, alongside common sense, are restored.

Every age has its own brand of heretics, some known and named and some working behind the scenes but all trying to undo the centuries of faith preserved by the Church. In some historical eras, certain individuals who believe that they are smarter than the pope tell everyone that the past is dead, and that changes are necessary if Catholics are to survive in the present. Most of these people are quite sincere. They really believe in what they are doing, at least until things start coming apart at the seams and they witness the damage they have done.

The heretics in Martin's time loved to debate theological matters about the nature of Christ, papal authority, and salvation. Most of them did not have the foggiest clue about what they were saying, so they yelled a lot and used their powers to abuse those Catholics loyal to the Church.

Seeing that such individuals were in power, Martin decided to avoid the confrontations that would result by his preaching and working in Poitiers. He looked for a place where he could pray and grow in union with God while others argued about matters of faith. He settled on an island in the Tyrrhenian Sea, at a place called Gallinaria, now Isola d'Albinga. There he lived as a hermit, giving praise and thanks to God — at least one sane voice to be raised in a wilderness of error.

In the year 361, however, his life as a hermit was interrupted when he learned news about Hilary. An imperial command had restored the holy bishop to Poitiers. Martin left the island and boarded a ship for Gaul. He went to Poitiers and once again met Hilary, filled with joy and with thanksgiving. He was not alone in greeting the return of the bishop. Other disciples arrived in Poitiers, and a community of monks was established there again, free to follow the old ways of the faith proven over the centuries.

Hilary, recognizing Martin as a truly chosen soul, welcomed him warmly. Discovering Martin's interest in the life of a hermit, and knowing that such a vocation, or calling, was from God, Hilary sent him out into the desert, to a place called Leguge. A famous Benedictine monastery would rise on the spot in time.

Martin was content with a small shelter there, away from the world and its noises. For ten years he lived as a hermit, praying, studying, and fasting alone. He was not exactly alone, however. More than a hundred holy men joined him in the retreat, all removed from the world and occupied with prayer. Martin left the hermitage on occasion, preaching in nearby towns and villages and converting hundreds of men and women.

Then, in 371, the bishop of Tours died, and the people of that city sent word to Martin, asking him to be their new spiritual leader. In those days the people of the various dioceses had a say in the appointment of their bishops. When a certain laxness and the usual sort of human nonsense began to bring unworthy men into power, the appointments came from Rome, as it is done today. Martin thanked the citizens of Tours but refused the honor that they wished to place upon his shoulders.

The people of Tours sent a second invitation; still, Martin was not moved by their pleas. He was a hermit and had no interest in becoming their bishop. Refused once more, the Tours leaders realized that it was time for some inventive thinking. They met and talked over the matter, coming up with a possible solution. They knew Martin, and they plotted a way of getting him to come to Tours. Once in the city, they believed he was theirs for life.

One of the city's most prosperous merchants, a man named Rusticus, hurried out into the desert to find Martin, as part of the plot. He was probably already known to the saint, perhaps even a friend. Rusticus told Martin that his wife was very ill, probably dying, and in need of the last rites (or anointing of the sick). Martin, of course, could not refuse the sacrament to Rusticus's wife, and he agreed to accompany the man back to the city.

When the men arrived in Tours, Martin found flowers and banners hanging everywhere. Crowds of citizens were on the streets, cheering him and welcoming him as the new bishop. He heard his name being shouted and hymns echoing everywhere. The way out of the city was also mobbed by men and women who had no intention of allowing him to leave Tours.

Martin had no choice in the matter. He went to the cathedral that very day, July 4, 371, and was consecrated as bishop of Tours. Even if he did not look terribly enthusiastic, the citizens of the city were satisfied. Martin was a holy man who knew obligations when he saw them. He would fulfill his role as bishop to the best of his ability because it was God's will.

Now he was not the usual type of bishop, and the people of Tours had to get used to that fact. He did not walk around in fancy robes or live in a grand house. Within weeks Martin was back out in the desert near Tours, this time at a place called Marmoutier. In an instant, of course, a great army of holy men arrived on the scene, other hermits who quickly gathered around him as a new community of praise rose in the wilderness.

He did not fail the city or the people. Because he was well

organized, focused only upon God, Martin was able to do everything necessary and still remain recollected, that is, he remained in the presence of God.

He also took part in the ongoing struggles over error and heresy. Martin of Tours was a staunch defender of the faith, and few opponents wanted to get caught in a debate with him. He had a quick and logical mind that could turn an enemy's word back on him. Martin was also learned enough to point out the stupidity or the errors of the heretics.

He was not a man who sought vengeance, however. When Martin learned that Emperor Maximus was being urged to behead a certain group of heretics, Martin raced to the imperial palace in Trier, in modern Germany. He pleaded his case before the emperor, crying out that the slaying of such individuals would serve no purpose. The executions were stopped because of Martin's eloquence.

Thus Martin of Tours continued his labors. He died on November 8, 397, in Candes in Tourine, France, after a visit to Rome, where he made a report on his labors. (Candes was another monastery founded by the saint during his travels.)

Now monasteries and convents are so much a part of the Catholic scene that people take them for granted. In the early centuries of the Church, however, such institutions did not exist. As with Martin's groups of hermits, the great monasteries developed from clusters of huts or groups of caves in the wild places of the earth.

Men such as Martin or Saint Anthony in Egypt were wise enough to know that human beings have to turn away from the world, even in their times, to discover God's presence. Out of their pioneering efforts came the great monastic traditions of the Church, raised to new heights by saints like Benedict and Bernard.

The Church has survived over the centuries because of the contemplatives — the men and women who are called to "live alone with The Alone [Almighty God]." Such men and women, through their prayers and penances, bring down the graces used by the parish priests, the apostles, and missionaries. Both forms of the religious life must be respected and kept alive if the Church is going to survive in the next centuries. Saint Martin of Tours understood the need in the early part of the faith.

He was declared a patron of France after his death. His feast day is November 11.

Chapter 17

Odilia

Children in certain historical periods, especially those born in the noble estates, were not considered as individuals of value. Today, for example, it is legal to dispose of babies yet unborn because they have been denied their rights as human beings by the courts. Some mothers, taking that sort of thinking to extremes, have resorted to terrible crimes. If they believe that their children are not perfect or are inconveniences in life, they simply kill them and then stand trial for murder. People hearing of such cases shake their heads and ask how a mother can do such a thing, forgetting that protection of human life in all stages is the only guarantee against such madness.

Saint Odilia, who was born at the end of the seventh century, was one of those unfortunate babies who did not live up to their parents' expectations. She was born in a place called Obernheim in the Alsace region of France, but she was born blind, a fact viewed as a disaster by the noble classes. The last thing any aristocratic family needed was a daughter who could not see.

Adalric (also called Aticus) was a noble of the region, and he expected his children to be perfect because he viewed them only as extensions of himself and his own line. When the servants showed him that his baby daughter could not see, he shocked everyone because he calmly ordered the servants to murder the child. It was very simple in his mind. A blind daughter was of no use to him. No one would marry her, and it would take all sorts of care and expense even to raise her to adulthood. Why spend time, energy, and money on someone who cannot repay the family?

Now Odilia's mother, the Lady Bereswinda, went almost mad with grief when she heard what Adalric planned. She had been living with this cold, calculating man for years, however, and she knew how to soften his harsh commands. With tears and pleas she kept after him until he finally agreed to send the baby away, to be raised by strangers. That, in itself, was not such a great idea, but at least that way the baby survived.

Adalric said that everything had to be done in secret, however. Complications could arise if people knew that he was abandoning his own child, who was an heiress of his line, someone who could lay claim to part of his lands. This nobleman was not only cruel but crafty about his relatives and human life.

Bereswinda had no intention of abandoning her daughter, and she agreed to his terms, knowing full well that she would not go along with the deception. She sent for a reliable peasant woman from the area and gave her the child. She also told the woman the truth about Odilia's identity and gave her enough money to assure that the woman and Odilia would live in some comfort. The peasant woman, kindhearted and saddened at the treatment of the child, took Odilia to a safe place in a nearby area called Baume-les-Dames.

For twelve years Odilia was raised by this woman, probably aware of her true rank and personal tragedy because the old foster mother could hardly have kept such a thing to herself. Besides, anyone belonging to the noble families of that era were easily recognized by the people around them. They were normally more delicately built than the peasants, fairer in coloring, with sharper profiles. The noble families chose their husbands and wives with care, keeping an eye on family traits and physical characteristics.

During her twelfth year, Odilia was placed in the convent at Baume. The peasant may have been unable to care for her, or else it was considered wise to have Odilia given a proper education. It is also possible that Lady Bereswinda watched her daughter from a distance, protecting her and deciding all things for her welfare. Whatever the reason, Odilia entered the convent.

She was baptized there by Saint Erhard, bishop of Ratisbon (now Regensburg), which means the truth about Odilia's birth was well known. He would not have gone to the convent to baptize just anyone. This twelve-year-old was someone special, and the holy bishop was there to start her on the road to Christ.

When Bishop Erhard touched Odilia's eyes with the holy chrism (oils) of baptism, she let out a cry of surprise and joy: Odilia was no longer blind! As her soul was now open to the graces of God, her eyes opened to the light. Word of the event spread like wildfire, naturally, and the bishop, hoping to put all things right again, went to Lord Adalric to tell him the good news.

Hugh, Adalric's son and Odilia's brother, had also heard of the miracle and had started plans for bringing the young woman home. That proved too much for Adalric, who resented interference even from his superiors, let alone his own offspring. He hit Hugh in a fit of anger and killed him.

Adalric, holding the broken body of his son and heir, faced the truth of all that had taken place as a result of his pride. God had performed a miracle in giving Odilia sight, the same young woman that Adalric had planned to slay because of her imperfection. The tragedy — and perhaps the reality of his role in all of it — struck home, and Adalric wept for his losses.

Now that spirit of repentance did not last long in a man of Adalric's character. He was the sole power in his small world, not required to answer to anyone for his crimes, particularly when they involved his own children. In no time at all he was back to his old ways.

He was kind to Odilia when she was returned to the palace, actually even affectionate and generous with gifts of clothing and jewels. Such displays were not signs of repentance, however. Adalric had figured out a way of using her miraculous sight to his own advantage. He announced those plans one day, intending to wed Odilia to a German baron. The marriage would take Odilia off his hands and would form an alliance that would benefit Adalric.

Odilia heard the news about her intended wedding and fled from the palace, with her father in hot pursuit. Filled with rage, he and his men chased her all over the countryside. Adalric was not one to be crossed by a daughter, miraculously cured or not, and he intended to make her understand that fact very well. She was caught by her father's men eventually and dragged into the great hall of the palace, where she expected to die like her kindly brother, Hugh. Adalric did plan to murder her, knowing he would never be able to change her mind. If she was sent to the German baron as a bride, she would have to be chained, gagged, and surrounded by armed men. She deserved death as far as he was concerned, because she wanted to stand in the way of his plans for the family.

Something changed Adalric's mind, however, or something stopped him from carrying out his murderous plans. No matter how hard he tried to kill Odilia he was unable to accomplish the deed. He wanted his daughter dead, and he wanted to do that personally; but he was miraculously stopped each time he thought he could commit the crime.

Broken by his own inability to murder his offspring, Adalric felt old and vulnerable. He listened to Odilia finally as she explained that God had restored her sight so that she could become the bride of Christ, not some German baron. She knew that she had been called to the religious life. This she told her father gently and quietly. Odilia was also supposed to found houses of prayer. Adalric must have been touched by her words and by God's grace, or else he was too exhausted to put up a fight about the matter. He gave her the family castle of Hackenburg, located in Odilienberg, in what is now Alsace, France.

Within a few years that castle had been transformed into an abbey, where women lived a cloistered life of prayer and penance. Odilia served as the abbess there, attracting many holy souls into Christ's service. She became well known in the area because she was granted visions and performed miracles for the ill and needy. She also expanded her monastic work, founding a new abbey at a site called Niedermunster.

No one has documented what ever became of Aldaric, whose personal ambitions and rages had proven so deadly. He disappeared from history at this stage, remembered only for his crimes upon God's chosen.

Odilia moved to Niedermunster to direct the developing abbey there, remaining in the new foundation until her death sometime around 720. Her body was returned to Odilienberg, where it was enshrined, and her feast day, the day of her death and entrance into heaven, was celebrated on December 13 soon after.

She was named the patroness of the Alsace region of France and the protectress of the blind. In Christian art, Saint Odilia is often depicted in her robes as an abbess, and she is shown holding a book. On the book are two human eyeballs, symbols of the miracle of her baptism.

Peter Claver

Chapter 18

Peter Claver

Sometimes, right out of the blue, so to speak, the most unlikely man or woman will end up accomplishing the most extraordinary acts of courage and faith. The grace of God makes all things possible, of course, but a human being able to do such feats or good works has to respond to God's grace by overcoming personal fears, dreads, and terrors in order to accomplish the particular mission set for him or her. Peter Claver was just such a rare individual. He managed to overcome himself in the face of really hideous conditions, and not on just one single grand occasion. His "heroic" deeds were performed every day of his life for more than half a century.

These "heroic" acts involved filth, disease, dungeons, slave pens, leprosy, and epidemics. He rose from his bed each day knowing that he was needed in the pits of horror around him, and he did not turn away in disgust or revulsion but went solemnly on his way in charity, seldom aided by the "good" Christians around him and sometimes threatened by them because he was "making waves."

He was born on a Catalonian farm near the village of Verdu, which was not too far from the great Spanish city of Barcelona, in 1580 or 1581. The farm and the daily life of caring for the animals and laboring in the fields would have trained him in discipline and perseverance. His parents, however, hoped for something more and sent him to the University of Barcelona, where he earned a degree by the age of twenty. An education of this nature was unusual for a farmer's son, of course, although the family could have been part of what they called "the landed gentry." Such people were members of older noble houses, no longer in power and probably no longer wealthy but still aware of their heritage and anxious to restore their family lines.

Whatever the reasons for sending Peter to the University of Barcelona, his parents agreed to allow him to turn aside from the world upon graduation. Peter Claver was not turning aside from the world, of course, but embracing the human condition in its most pitiful states. He entered the Jesuit novitiate (a type of training seminary) and was eventually assigned to Montesione College on the island of Majorca, where a great saint was waiting to open heaven's doors to him.

That saint was Alphonsus Rodríguez, who actually did open doors and gateways. The elderly holy man served as a porter, the one who welcomed visitors and tradesmen to the monastery and college. Now it may seem odd that a saint of such distinction and fame should be assigned the lowly position of porter in a remote monastery, but such a strange situation certainly follows the pattern of human behavior seen everywhere since the world began.

To begin with, Alphonsus Rodríguez was so thrilled to be a Jesuit that he accepted any assignment given to him, having entered the order at a somewhat advanced age. Secondly, he was humble and holy and felt no need to describe his beautiful spiritual life to his companions, unless the grace of God prompted him to do so for a reason. He spent his days and nights opening doors, welcoming guests and students, and counseling all of the young men sent to him by God. Peter Claver was such a chosen young man.

Now most of the other monks and visitors were quite unaware of the treasure in their midst, Saint Alphonsus. Some viewed him as an elderly nitwit who performed his small tasks with care. Others found him a bit odd, especially in matters of obedience (as he believed that obedience was the primary role of a religious). Making such superficial judgments, of course, his fellow monks did not bother to ask about Alphonsus' personal experiences in the spiritual life. Why would they? They had problems of their own to worry about each day.

Only when Alphonsus died in 1617 did it dawn on anyone in the college that they had been in the company of a saint. When thousands of mourners arrived for his funeral, including high-ranking dignitaries of the Church and government, his fellow priests began to understand the true scope of his influence and the depths of his sanctity. By then it was too late for any of them to pay him respect, but Alphonsus did not mind. He showered the community with miracles from heaven.

Peter Claver spent three critical years of formation in the company of Alphonsus Rodríguez. They talked every day, and Alphonsus — who had discerned Peter's special vocation, or calling

— urged the young man to serve God in the New World, another name for places including North and South America. There he would perform all the "heroic" deeds of which he was capable. As Peter studied and grew in God's grace, Alphonsus repeated his urgings and worked to prepare the young man for the mission at hand.

In 1610, all of the years of discernment on Majorca came to flower. Peter Claver, following Alphonsus' spiritual instructions, volunteered for the missions and was sent to Cartagena, in Colombia, then a Spanish territory. When he arrived there he started his last training session before ordination to the priesthood, and he also learned a truly dreadful lesson about human beings. He discovered just how brutal and vile the human race could be when power and greed ruled over all.

Colombia is a modern nation on the northwest corner of South America, bounded on the northeast by the Caribbean Sea. The Spanish conquered the area, putting the territory under their control by 1563, enslaving the local Indian groups and seeking the gold mines of the region. El Dorado, the fabled mine that has filled men with greed for centuries, was supposedly in Colombia, as it was rumored to have existed elsewhere in the New World.

Following the conquistadores, the merciless armies of Spanish soldiers and explorers who ravaged the lands and peoples of the New World, a new breed arrived to capitalize on the gains made. These were businessmen and adventurers bent on carving out their own financial empires and quite willing to exploit the native populations in order to amass fortunes.

The native populations, however, did not fit into the Spanish plans as easily as it was hoped. These were Indians used to living close to the earth and roaming free through the beautiful, exotic wilderness of the Colombia region. The Spanish forced them into mines and into large fields of agriculture, and there they collapsed and died. Hope fled, and the Indians quite simply lay down and turned their hearts away from their grim life, knowing that only evil surrounded them and awaited them each day. Whippings, beatings, and other Spanish tortures only made the situation worse. The more they were abused the quicker the native populations sickened and died.

The Spanish, of course, had to do something even they considered drastic if their grand plans were going to succeed. After much debate and furor they decided upon importing boatloads of black slaves that were available from the continent of Africa. Such men and women could be brought aboard ship, chained in the hold, and fed only the minimum to keep them alive during the voyage. Those that managed to make the long journey with their bodies and souls intact could be put to work. The survival of the fittest was the rule here, and the Spanish did not worry about the black men and women who perished on board the dreadful slave ships. They paid only two ecus (the monetary standard at the time) for each slave, and they could sell each one for two hundred ecus in Cartagena.

Peter Claver, being trained in the Jesuit seminary by Father Alphonsus de Sandoval, a true apostle of charity, saw the slave ships and the hideous pens and dungeons in which the imported men and women were kept in the city. He declared himself "the slave of the Negroes forever." This was no idle boast or romantic fancy. He was timid and humble by nature, but the agony of the slaves, so heartrending, so hideous, transformed him into a whirlwind of activity and strength.

Peter Claver was ordained a priest in 1615 and given a free hand with his mission, although he was probably cautioned by older, more experienced priests about the arrogance and cruelty of the Spanish aristocrats. He started out in a well-organized fashion, going in the pilot boat (the vessel of the Cartagena harbor master) to meet each arriving slave ship. There he forced the ship's crews to open the hold, exposing the human cargo that had been so brutalized by the hardships of the long voyage, the darkness, and cramped space. The slaves were half crazed by the time they reached Cartagena, and Peter Claver went to each one of them personally, giving them food and water, binding their wounds, and soothing them with kindness. In order to make even more direct and personal contact, he used translators who were familiar with the various African dialects.

In the city's holding pens, he brought food, medicine, brandy, and tobacco to the slaves. Peter even went into the mines and plantations to inspect conditions and care for the slaves held there. It is recorded that he converted more than three hundred thousand in his ministry and heard five thousand confessions a year. He is also reported as having baptized as many as three million souls.

When a particular landowner or mine director refused to ease his treatment of the slaves under his control, he found himself face to face with Peter Claver. The saint moved into the mine or plantation owned by the tyrant, living with the slaves and confronting the Spanish hour by hour.

Now this type of behavior did not win him many friends among the Spanish, as his older religious companions had probably warned him. Not only the landowners and mine directors hated the sight of him. He had enemies even in the Church, where some accused him of blasphemy. These odd churchmen actually declared that the slaves scarcely possessed souls and were therefore unworthy of the sacraments that Peter so lovingly lavished on them.

The saint also saw society matrons leave a church when he arrived on the altar. They were displaying their sensitivity to his work, declaring by their actions that he had become infected with all sorts of terrible diseases through his contact with the slaves. He responded to this sort of mindless hysteria by redoubling his efforts.

Sailors and travelers found him a welcome patron when they arrived in the city port. Peter Claver nursed lepers and victims of St. Anthony's fire, a painful skin disease of the area. He also performed miracles for those in his care and announced prophecies that were proven genuine. As a result of all this increased work, and the obvious signs of God's favor, the Spanish of Cartagena slowly came to realize the mission of Peter Claver. Some even admitted that Cartagena was a cesspool of cruelty and vice, a city spared God's wrath only because Peter Claver lived within its borders. He was called the "Oracle of Cartagena," as more and more of the high-ranking Spanish flocked to aid him in his work.

Then the plague of 1650 struck in the region, and Peter Claver went among the thousands of stricken to bring comfort and medical care. He caught the disease and tried to keep working but was soon confined to his small cell (the name given in the past for a monk's room), where a single slave took care of him. For four years the saint suffered alone, as the people of Cartagena, busy rebuilding their lives, forgot all about him. He died alone on September 8, 1654, and suddenly everyone in the city recognized the loss.

A massive civic funeral was held, attended by thousands, and Peter Claver was laid to rest in Cartagena. Both Peter and Alphonsus Rodríguez were canonized by Pope Leo XIII in 1888, united on the altars of the Church as they had been in their human roles. In 1896, Saint Peter Claver was declared the patron of all Catholic missions to the Negroes, or blacks. His feast day is celebrated on September 9.

Thomas More

Chapter 19

Thomas More

Most people have heard about the historical events called the crusades. These started as military campaigns to free the Holy Land — where Christ had walked — and the surrounding territories from the control of the Muslims. In today's history books these crusades are too often portrayed as cruel raids by Westerners on innocent populations. Now, not all of the crusades were honorable, and the Christian armies did not practice the mercy of the Lord in all their dealings with the people they called "infidels." Still, Saint Louis of France (Louis IX) and others committed themselves for very good and noble purposes: to free Christian slaves from their prisons and to open Jerusalem once again to the followers of Christ.

While people understand or at least know about the crusades — either from the traditional historical view or the new, revised version — few recognize the impact that these military adventures had on the Western world. Contact with the ancient city of Constantinople, the works of famous Islamic scholars, and the glorious architecture of the Middle Eastern cities, startled the crusaders, who began to collect books and art treasures, carrying them back to Europe at the close of each campaign.

The end result, of course, was the historical period called the Renaissance, the rebirth of philosophy and the arts. The past, so carefully preserved in Constantinople and in the Middle Eastern lands, burst upon Europe like a sun, prompting scholars to study the Greek philosophers and the arts of the Classical Age.

Saint Thomas More was an Englishman who benefited from this end result of the crusades. When the works of the Greek masters — Aristotle, Plato, and others — became popular, his own brilliant mind absorbed their philosophical goals and transformed them along Christian ideals. Had Thomas not become a martyr to the desires of his king, preferring death to dishonor by approving sin, he would still be remembered as one of the leading philosophers of his day. Because of his martyrdom, Thomas is venerated as a saint of the Church.

Thomas More was born in London, England, on February 6, 1478. He was the sole surviving son of Sir John More and his first wife, Agnes. He was educated in a school on Threadneedle Street in London and at the age of thirteen became a page for Cardinal John Morton, the archbishop of Canterbury. Cardinal Morton also served as the lord chancellor of England, second only to the king at the time, Henry VII.

Young men of the upper classes were sent as pages, messengers, and assistants to the houses of prominent lords. It was a rather good form of education because such pages watched their elders govern the state, conduct legal affairs, and display the standards of behavior for the station, or position in the world.

Thomas was described by Erasmus (the famous Renaissance philosopher) as somewhat short in stature but with "limbs formed with such perfect symmetry as to leave nothing to be desired." Erasmus added: "His complexion is white, his face fair rather than pale and though by no means ruddy, a faint blush of pink appears beneath the whiteness of his skin. His hair is dark brown or brownish black. His eyes are grayish blue, with some spots, a kind which betokens singular talent. . . . His countenance is in harmony with his character, being always expressive of an amiable joyousness, and even an incipient laughter and, so to speak, candidly, it is better framed for gladness. . . . He seems born and framed for friendship, and is a most faithful and enduring friend. . . . No one is less led by the opinions of the crowd, yet no one departs less from common sense."

The joy and fierce loyalty of Thomas More touched everyone while he was of a young age. His ability to ignore "the opinions of the crowd" would come later in his life much to the shock and horror of the English government.

Cardinal Morton was certainly impressed with the teen-aged Thomas, and he sent him to Oxford University in 1492. Thomas's father, of course, had to provide his son with an allowance, but it was doled out in such meager amounts that Thomas couldn't afford many pleasures. That fact, naturally, kept him in his room, studying. One of his classes while in Oxford was Greek, that language then being considered essential to a man of learning. Thomas also spoke and read French and Latin, studied history and mathematics, and became quite good at playing the flute and the viol.

He spent two years at Oxford and then returned to London to study law at the New Inn, moving to Lincoln's Inn, another law school, in 1496. While a student, Thomas lectured in law and was given other ranks by the faculty. At the same time he was writing poetry in Latin and in English and studying the Greek philosophers.

Spiritually, Thomas More practiced a rather severe style of penance and spent many hours in prayer. He probably considered a religious vocation, but his mission was in the world, and he was well equipped by natural abilities and the grace of God to perform such tasks.

In 1501, he became a member of the bar, which means he was certified as a lawyer. In 1504, he was elected as a member of Parliament, which brought him into conflict between the House of Commons and King Henry VII. The king was regarded as the cheapest monarch ever to take the English throne. Thomas attacked the new taxation being laid upon the land by the king, getting it reduced by more than eighty thousand pounds (about one hundred twenty thousand U.S. dollars in 1995). Now that brought him to Henry's attention quickly.

Thomas had been very careful to attack the amount of money involved in the taxation demands without once insulting the name or the character of Henry. That, as someone said later, saved Thomas's head. The king retaliated, of course, by putting Sir John More, Thomas's father, in the Tower of London and making him pay a hundred-pound fine for a nonexistent crime. Sir John did not take it badly, being used to the ways of the throne.

Taking note of the power of kings and worried about his father having to pay for his own action, Thomas proceeded with his own personal life. He married a woman named Jane Colt in 1505. A son named John and three daughters — Margaret, Elizabeth, and Cecilia — were born to the couple. He lost Jane in 1511, a cruel blow for him because she had been a charming, gentle young woman. In time, knowing his own needs and those of his household, Thomas married a widow named Alice Middleton, described as seven years older than he was — plain, with common sense, little education, and a marvelous flair for housekeeping.

When Henry VII died, his second son, Henry VIII, took the throne. By this time, More was a well-known lawyer, respected by one and all, and considered a prudent, honest man, which meant that he was somewhat unique for his time.

England not only had a handsome young king on the throne but a new cardinal archbishop of Canterbury. His name was Thomas Wolsey, a rather cunning churchman who replaced Morton as lord chancellor as well. In 1510, More was made undersheriff of London, and four years later was sent to Flanders to negotiate over a six-month period on behalf of English merchantmen. In his masterpiece, *Utopia*, More speaks of that embassy. In the next years he performed similar negotiating journeys, while the *Utopia* was being read throughout Europe. Everywhere More was hailed for his brilliance, his legal skills, and his ideals.

By 1518, More, in fact, was a royal councilor and an honored member of the court. He accompanied King Henry VIII to France in 1520, where the monarchs, Francis I of France and Emperor Charles V, met with him. Because of the splendor of the various camps, the site of the meeting was forever after called "the Field of the Cloth of Gold."

Upon returning to England, Thomas More was knighted and made an assistant royal treasurer, and one honor was piled upon another in the following years. He became the speaker of the House of Commons, high steward of Cambridge, and chancellor of Lancaster.

Henry VIII, handsome, robust, charming, was also receiving praise and respect. He was proving himself shrewd in governing the nation and in destroying enemies of the English crown. At the same time, however, his own mental abilities were on display before all Christendom, as he wrote in 1521 a book called *Assertio Septem Sacramentorum* (*Defense of the Seven Sacraments*), a repudiation of Martin Luther and a defense of the Church's sacraments. Pope Leo X received the work with joy and, in return, gave Henry the title of *Fidei Defensor* (*Defender of the Faith*). This papal title remains to this day with the throne of England, even though Catholicism is no longer the state religion there.

More's manor, built in Chelsea in 1523, became the gathering place of the intellectuals of the age. The manor had beautiful gardens facing the Thames, and crowds arrived for meals and hours of discussion. The king often came unannounced, dining and strolling in the gardens with Thomas. The saint, however, was not dazzled by his popularity and placed little faith in Henry's good wishes. As he explained it: "If my head should win him a castle in France, it should not fail to go."

The life of Thomas and that of the nation changed for all time in 1527, when Henry met a woman named Anne Boleyn. Although married to Catherine of Aragon, Henry managed to sire children from other women, including Anne's sister Mary. Queen Catherine's surviving child was a daughter, also called Mary.

Now much has been said about the six wives of Henry VIII, although few people know the details of their brief reigns. The first of his wives was Catherine of Aragon, a Spanish-born princess who was the widow of Arthur, Henry's older brother. Arthur did not live to take the throne, being sickly. His crown and his wife in name only — the marriage between Arthur and Catherine was never consummated because of Arthur's illness — became Henry's in 1509. In 1527 or 1528, Henry asked Catherine for an annulment of the marriage, on the grounds that she had been Arthur's wife. She refused, knowing that her daughter, Mary, would be declared illegitimate. Henry had Catherine placed in a remote castle, under primitive conditions, but she held to her convictions until she died from her sufferings in 1533.

Anne Boleyn became Henry's queen in the same year, although the English used other names and titles when they spoke of her, all of them rather unpleasant. She bore Henry only one child, a daughter, Elizabeth, and then found herself in the Tower of London on trumped-up charges. There she was beheaded in 1536, thus being called by some "Anne of the Thousand Days."

Jane Seymour followed her to the throne in the same year, fondly named "the little nun" by Henry. She died giving birth to Prince Edward, who became Edward VI, in 1547.

Anne of Cleves was brought to England as the next wife, but she was an educated woman, sophisticated, and given to her own ideas. Henry proved no match for her character, as she dared to tell Henry face to face that he was called "the wife butcher" in other European countries. The two were divorced in 1540, Anne having lasted only a few months as the royal consort! She and Henry (who was very generous to her after the divorce) remained good friends.

After the separation and settlement between Henry and Anne, Catherine Howard was named queen of England, and Henry doted on her. She, in turn, had affairs with others in the palace and laughed at Henry's weight and age. Catherine was beheaded in the Tower of London in 1542. She was followed by the last of Henry's wives, Catherine Parr, who was fortunate enough to outlive him.

When Anne Boleyn thus arrived on the scene, she set into motion political and religious matters that would claim countless victims and alienate the English people from the Church. One of the first to fall because of Henry's desire for an annulment of his marriage to his wife Catherine was Cardinal Wolsey. (An annulment is a declaration that a marriage is not valid, that is, not a true marriage.) Cardinal Wolsey was removed as lord chancellor of England, and Thomas More was given that post in 1529, the first English layman to have it.

He was thus caught in many levels of conflict. The Lutherans were gaining ground in Europe, and Thomas had to enforce England's laws about heresy. Henry was denied his annulment from Catherine of Aragon and was about to tear apart the English Church. Knowing this, Thomas remained silent for as long as he could but then resigned his position as lord chancellor in 1532.

Reduced to a much lower standard of living, and removed from the royal favor he had enjoyed for so long, Thomas secluded himself in his Chelsea manor. He remained there with his family for a year and a half, safe from the turmoil. Henry was attacking the churches and monasteries in England, closing them down and taking possession of their treasures. He turned his back on the pope and named himself the supreme head of the Church in the British Isles.

Anne Boleyn was crowned as queen, and Thomas stayed away from the ceremony, but other leaders wanted to see him make a public announcement of where he stood. Thomas was therefore summoned to appear before a council and rather easily set their charges aside, saying his personal feelings had been expressed to the king already. He had no intention of repeating a conversation that was a private matter involving the king.

Some of More's friends, however, felt honor-bound to warn Thomas of what he would face if he persisted. He replied: "Is that all . . . ? Then in good faith is there no more difference between your grace and me, but that I shall die today and you tomorrow."

In March 1534, the Act of Succession, a command that English citizens had to swear allegiance to the children of Henry and Anne Boleyn as the heirs to the throne, was issued throughout England.

Thomas More was summoned to take the oath concerning the Act of Succession, and when he refused was hauled into custody. Within four days he was in the Tower of London.

King Henry VIII, with Anne at his side, was about to crush his enemies, even though such men were holy servants or bishops of the Church. The land grants that Thomas had received as part of his royal favor were confiscated, and conditions of his imprisonment harshened by his guards.

He suffered from constant bronchial problems as well as stomach cramps; but he maintained a good humor, especially in front of his family. They wept, knowing that Thomas could not compromise with the truth, which was actually rather simple and easy to defend.

Henry VIII was not the supreme head of the Church; neither was he the savior of England. He was a middle-aged monarch, corrupted by absolute power and willing to destroy anyone or anything that stood in his way. He loved Anne, no doubt, to the point that others claimed she bewitched him; but he could turn on her in an instant when she proved unable to give him an heir. A prince of his blood was vital to Henry to avoid civil war in the land, and much of his fury and cruelty can be traced to this fact.

Thomas, watching from afar, saw all these aspects at play in Henry's personality. He weighed them, however, against the truth of the faith and refused to say or do anything that would give the king encouragement. In his cell in the Tower of London, Thomas was faced with his successor as lord chancellor, a man named Thomas Cromwell. Cromwell had been sent to interview the saint about his views, little dreaming that he too would follow Thomas More into the Tower and onto the executioner's block. Thomas More only admitted to being the "king's loyal servant" during that interview.

When it was discovered that Thomas had been exchanging letters with another famous prisoner in the Tower, Saint John Fisher, the former bishop of Rochester who refused to deny his allegiance to the Holy Father, the guards took away his books and writing papers. He had been spending his nights and days composing religious treatises (or manuals and studies) and works on philosophy. Thomas had also spent many hours in prayer, knowing the end was near and marvelously calm about its approach.

On July 1, 1535, Thomas More was taken to Westminster Hall to be charged with high treason. A young man named Richard Rich, who had once wanted to be Thomas's protégé (a kind of assistant or pupil), was the chief witness against him, making up such really stupid lies that his perjury (lying under oath) was obvious. Rich recited all kinds of things that Thomas was supposed to have said. Those present in the courtroom were aware of the fact that Thomas was a lawyer and a judge, a gifted writer who well knew the power of words. He was too trained and too cautious to have said anything of the kind, particularly to a greedy little nobody like Rich.

The verdict, of course, could not be altered by the recognition of perjury and lies. Every man in that trial understood what Henry VIII demanded of them. If they did not rid the land of this stern defender of the Catholic faith they would join him in the Tower.

The verdict was guilty, as expected by one and all. The sentence was death by hanging at a place called Tyburn Hill, which became the setting for the terrible martyrdom of Catholic priests during Elizabeth I's reign. Protestants died there as well in the reign of Elizabeth's older sister, Mary. Henry VIII, however, perhaps prompted by memories of happier days, or perhaps fearful of Thomas's popularity with the English people, changed the sentence. Thomas More was to face beheading in a private court of the Tower of London. One year later, Anne Boleyn died in the same prison, also beheaded.

Faced with the end, Thomas regarded the coming execution with good humor and with calm. He did not look at the separation of his head from his body as a good reason for becoming hysterical. The event was merely the outcome of a long line of happenings, leading directly to this final confrontation. As he had predicted long before, this was how Henry rewarded his friends. The king was not seeking to gain "another castle in France," but Thomas's life was viewed as worthless. He could be slain so that Anne Boleyn would feel safer on the throne.

Thomas More was beheaded on Tower Hill just before nine on the morning of July 6, 1535. Using the right of all condemned prisoners to speak before the executioner, he simply announced that he was "the King's good servant but God's first." These words were carefully chosen. They did not insult Henry VIII, who might have retaliated against Thomas's family after the execution. They did explain the saint's refusal to join the crowds in their error, a trait that Erasmus clearly showed in his description of Thomas's character. Error was error, whether committed by the uneducated rabble or by the crowned heads of the nation. Thomas picked no quarrel with the king, but he did not go meekly into eternity without reminding Henry and his fellow countrymen that they had denied the faith and now stood in error. He died willingly to bring home that truth, and because of his sense of honor.

His decapitated body was given to his stricken family for burial in the Church of St. Peter Ad Vincula in London. His severed head, however, was first boiled in water and then stuck on a pole on London Bridge. The Traitor's Gate of the Tower of London also displayed the heads of the condemned. They remained as grisly reminders to the people for thirty days and then were thrown into the Thames River. At the end of the month, however, Margaret Thomas's oldest daughter bribed the man in charge of such ghastly relics. When he took down Thomas's head he did not throw it away but gave it to her for safekeeping.

The head was discovered in 1842 in a leaden box stored in St. Dunstan's Church in Canterbury. The Jesuits at the Stonyhurst Monastery have other relics of the saint, as the last male heir of the More family line, a man also named Thomas, became a Jesuit. The saint's hair shirt, a very uncomfortable garment worn next to the skin for the sake of penance, was taken out of the Tower the day before Thomas died and is now in an Augustinian convent. The British Museum displays Thomas's letters, and there he is known as Sir Thomas More. His portraits, including the one painted by the famous artist Holbein, are still in existence and much treasured. And Thomas still resides in a way in Chelsea, overlooking his beloved Thames River. A statue of him can be found there just in front of the space once occupied by his famous manor.

On December 29, 1886, Thomas More was declared Blessed by Pope Leo XIII. His writings continued to influence people of all faiths because of their clarity and vivid truths. His book *Utopia*, actually a fictionalized adventure of a man named Raphael Hythlodaye, depicts his own era and pokes gentle fun at his contemporaries and the times. His autobiographical works form a wonderful picture of his mind and heart. Thus generations coming after him have not lost the blessed reasoning and calm that pervaded his life and death. In 1935, Thomas More was canonized by Pope Pius XI. His feast day is June 22.

Veronica

Chapter 20

Veronica

One of the most enduring Catholic religious traditions that have survived over the centuries is the devotion called the Stations of the Cross, also named the Way of the Cross (*Via Crucis*) or the Sorrowful Way (*Via Dolorosa*). In the city of Jerusalem there are fourteen separate locations identified as the actual sites associated with Christ's passion. These sites were designated by the first Christians in the city, some of whom had actually watched our Lord's passion, and maintained throughout the centuries by the faithful.

The sites are on the pilgrimage route through the city, traditionally referred to as the Via Dolorosa. Following in Christ's footsteps, touching the stones and the walls of the ancient streets and buildings allowed the early followers of Jesus the blessed opportunity of sharing in the reality of his crucifixion, and the custom became popular immediately.

In the earliest times, and during the eras of the persecution of the Church, the Christian pilgrims had to be very prudent and cautious when making the stations, but they kept the devotion alive. With the passing of the years, the Stations of the Cross did not fade but actually became more popular.

Many pilgrims who traveled all the way to Jerusalem were so moved by the experience that they duplicated the Way of the Cross in their own European cities, thus the devotion gained popularity outside of the Holy Land. The Way of the Cross depicts Christ being condemned to death by Pontius Pilate and then follows the Passion to the Crucifixion, descent from the cross and the placing of Jesus in the tomb. Each of the significant encounters was marked by an image in the early days, a practice still in use today.

In the fifteenth century, an Englishman named William Wey used the term "station" when referring to such sacred locations. In 1505, a

Belgian named Peter Sterchx wrote the first book about the stations, setting the pattern for the devotion as it is practiced now. Saint Leonard of Port Maurice popularized the devotion, and the Franciscans — who were given charge of the actual holy sites associated with Christ's life in 1342 — received permission to place the stations in all of their churches.

In the modern form of the Way of the Cross, paintings or carved panels are hung on the walls of parishes throughout the world. These depictions allow Catholic worshipers to make a spiritual pilgrimage on the Via Dolorosa, reliving the passion of Christ and receiving graces even though they are unable to go in person to Jerusalem.

One of the Stations of the Cross, the sixth one in the devotional series, introduces the world to a very mysterious, courageous woman. According to one story, she was a matron of Jerusalem who stepped out of the crowd and held up a cloth so that Jesus' face could be wiped free of the blood and sweat of his torments. When she finished her act of compassion and devotion, the cloth had been altered. The face of Christ was miraculously imprinted on the material, complete with the crown of thorns and the wounds caused by this cruel headpiece.

Saint John wrote about this woman and about her ministration, or act of care, to Jesus in the face of Roman soldiers and the jeers of the nonbelievers in the crowd. John does not identify the woman, but ever after scholars have tried to place a name on her. As a result, many legends and traditions have grown around this sixth station and the unknown figure. She is called Veronica today. That is not a Hebrew name but is the result of two Latin words: *vera icon*, meaning "true image."

Some scholars believe that Veronica was actually Saint Martha, the sister of Lazarus and Mary. This is a possibility, of course, because nothing would have stopped Martha from trying to make Jesus more comfortable, even in that terrible hour. There is no historical documentation for such a choice, so Martha remains doubtful in the minds of others.

Another tradition states that Veronica was a matron of Jerusalem, as John claimed, an older woman, probably widowed. She is supposed to have been called to Rome by Emperor Tiberius, who reigned from 14 to 37. There she is also supposed to have used the "true image" to cure Tiberius of a fatal disease.

Now historians will readily admit that Tiberius probably had every disease known to man. Bitter and unhappy over being forced to marry the daughter of Emperor Augustus, Tiberius went into self-imposed exile in the Greek isles before Augustus died. Tiberius was the son of Tiberius Claudius Nero and Livia, who divorced her husband and became Augustus's second wife. Livia was a woman who plotted to see her son on the imperial throne and who kept her son under constant control in order to put him into the right position for inheriting power. Tiberius fled from her and her influences.

In the Greek isles, he lived rather wickedly, even for that era; he was drunk and on drugs much of the time, and he suffered from diseases that he picked up along the way. It seems unlikely that Veronica would have cured such a human monster with the sacred relic, but she may not have been given a choice.

After the legendary miraculous cure of Tiberius, Veronica is supposed to have lived in Rome, near Saints Peter and Paul. She gave the sacred image to Pope Saint Clement for safekeeping.

In another tradition, Veronica was the wife of a man named Zacchaeus. She went to Rome with him and then to a small town that was known later as Quiercy in Gaul (which became France). There she and her husband became hermits. In this version, Veronica is associated with Saint Martial and his apostolic labors.

In yet another tradition, Veronica traveled to France, alone, and there she preached and did charitable works and then died. A shrine in Bordeaux was erected over her grave.

So many traditions, all undocumented, leave Veronica as mysterious as she appears in the Stations of the Cross. Her real name, rank, and social status are unknown, but she emerges from the Way of the Cross in a very startling and beautiful manner. She is the *vera icon*, the true image of the Christian as she halts the procession in the street in order to comfort Jesus.

Christ was not alone but surrounded by Roman soldiers who had little love for the Jews and were probably annoyed by having to take a condemned criminal through the crowded streets. It was never safe to cross one of these Romans, but Veronica stood her ground in order to comfort Jesus as best she could.

In doing just this, Veronica adds a tender, intimate, and totally personal moment to the Via Dolorosa. She stepped in front of the procession so that she could offer consolation. Certainly the Roman guards would not have been alarmed by her sudden appearance. She was no crazed revolutionary intending to rescue Jesus and to slay them all. She could even have reminded the soldiers of their own mothers, who were quite probably the only decent women these men had known over the years. Soldiers were not invited into the homes of upper-class people in those days. The Romans watched, perhaps wondering who would offer them a similar kindness when they faced their own ends on some battlefield of the empire. The procession halted and Veronica knelt to wipe the face of Jesus. It was a very simple act, but she performed it with courage and devotion.

Veronica becomes a woman not so mysterious, not so distant or obscure. She represents all that is good in human beings, the spark of bravery that is fed by compassion and faith. Her name says it all. She stands as a "true image" of what Christ asked all men and women to become in his name. Saint Veronica's feast day is celebrated on July 12.

Now doth the fiery sun
  decline;
Thou Unity eternal shine;
Thou Trinity, thy blessings
  pour,
And make our hearts with
  love run o'er.
Thee in the hymns of morn
  we praise:
To thee our voice at eve we
  raise;
Oh, grant us with thy saints
  on high;
Thee through all time to
  glorify.

Iam sol recedit Ignitus
First Vespers
Feast of the Holy Trinity

More "Heroes with Halos!"

If you enjoyed the "heroes with halos" you met in **Lives of the Saints You Should Know Volume 2**, you'll want to read **Lives of the Saints You Should Know Volume 1**! From St. Francis of Assisi to Mother Frances Cabrini, these lively, informative biographies present more vibrant, exciting individuals who lived and loved their lives of Faith. Included are Thomas Becket, Agatha, Genevieve, Clare, John Neuman, Pius X, and many more...such as Blessed Damien of Molokai and Edith Stein! Order your copy today!

Lives of the Saints You Should Know
By Margaret and Matthew Bunson
0-87973-**576**-7, paper, $7.95, 150 pp.

Available at bookstores. MasterCard, VISA, and Discover customers can order direct from **Our Sunday Visitor** by calling **1-800-348-2440**. Or, send payment plus $3.95 shipping/handling to **Our Sunday Visitor**.

 Our Sunday Visitor
200 Noll Plaza
Huntington, IN 46750
1-800-348-2440

Your Source for Discovering the Riches of the Catholic Faith

A63BBCBP